ACCELERATING AUTOMATIC

Lead Transformation, Inspire Performance, Coach Discipline, and Tap Into Team Flow

TIM WIGHAM

authorHOUSE®

AuthorHouse™ UK
1663 Liberty Drive
Bloomington, IN 47403 USA
www.authorhouse.co.uk
Phone: 0800 047 8203 (Domestic TFN)
*   +44 1908 723714 (International)*

Published by AuthorHouse 04/15/2020

ISBN: 978-1-7283-5215-2 (sc)
ISBN: 978-1-7283-5214-5 (e)

Print information available on the last page.

This book is printed on acid-free paper.

Foreword

Tim is not just a regular blogger he's a serial thinker on human potential and the notion of continuous improvement as a force for good in all aspects of life. Based on first-hand experience in the military, the sporting arena, and various large energy corporations, Tim's collection of thought leadership is a personal quest to lay out a blueprint which helps leaders to create the optimal conditions for performance improvement.

Accelerating Automatic steps beyond inspiration to propose that blueprint. It is another triumphant blend of curiosity, acute observation, personal reflection, deep insight and pragmatism. Tim's simple and sensible model provides a frame of reference for us all to consider, as we strive to adapt to contemporary challenges in a complex world.

Chris Milliner
– Director of Performance Climate System (PCS)

Contents

This book is for my wife
ANGELA WIGHAM
a truly fast learner!

Thanks for inspiring through action. Your energy, and your commitment to our family and community, is hard to match.

"I will prepare, and some day my chance will come."
—Abraham Lincoln

Introduction

Over the last ten years, I have completely immersed myself in the business of accelerated improvement, supporting leaders and teams in upstream oil and gas, to unlock their potential and to exceed their expectations.

I have also focused on accelerating my own improvement in the sport of CrossFit, applying the principles of "acceleration to automatic" in the areas of nutrition, preparation, training, and recovery.

In parallel, I have read and listened to hundreds of performance-related books while also writing three of my own.

I strongly believe that any competent individual or team can unlock full potential by implementing the right system to the point where best practice is automatic.

This requires mindset, method, and mood.

Mindset is led by leadership! It involves openness to possibility, openness to objective assessment, openness to coaching, and a belief in better. It includes optimism and resilience in equal measure. Mindset is critical for initiative, and it is essential for acceleration to automatic.

Method is system discipline. It requires an uncompromising adherence to proven process, even when it is the last thing anyone feels like doing. The process may not be perfect, but it certainly works. Method allows repeated practice to become automatic.

Mood describes the prevailing performance climate. It includes intangible but invaluable behaviours and deliverables which maintain the right atmosphere for team excellence. Mood is the magic which helps mindset and method drive mastery, which is essentially the stage of unconscious competence where high performance is automatic.

Model: This simple model illustrates the connection I have experienced supporting teams at the front line and in my own life while striving to become a better human. Champions and champion teams tend to model the mastery of that integration of mindset, method, and mood.

Mastery: This is the sweet spot, where the hard work pays off and ten years turns into overnight success. It is sustainable if the contributing elements are kept in balance and maintained at an optimal level.

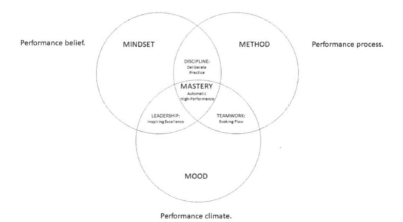

Performance belief.   MINDSET   METHOD   Performance process.

DISCIPLINE:
Deliberate
Practice

MASTERY
Automatic
High-Performance

LEADERSHIP: TEAMWORK:
Inspiring Excellence   Evoking Flow

MOOD

Performance climate.

This book expands on these three elements to provide extensive reference material for those of us who believe that average is an excuse, and better is possible.

I selected the quote by Abraham Lincoln at the start of this performance guide because it focuses on the process over which we do have direct control. It reminds us that it is by doing everything within our power to be the best we can be, that we will succeed, and that by continually "showing up" we will put ourselves in the best position to achieve the extraordinary when our chance arrives. Lincoln himself was the embodiment of resilience, determination, and a never-quit mindset.

1843—He ran for Congress. He lost.
1846—He ran for Congress again. He won and moved to Washington.
1848—He ran for re-election to Congress. He lost.
1854—He ran for the Senate of the United States. He lost.
1858—He ran for the Senate again. He lost again.
1860—Abraham Lincoln is elected president of the United States.

In the year 2020, Lincoln is generally regarded as one of the greatest presidents of the United States.

I have written this structured guide to accelerate the improvement journey for aspirant leaders and teams. I believe that competent teams can master their craft with a genuine willingness to strengthen the collective mindset, implement a proven method, and maintain the optimal mood for excellence. It takes extra effort, but this effort is exponentially rewarded over time, especially when the effort no longer feels like extra effort because the right habits become automatic.

Enjoy the guide and own your journey.

DIAL 1

MINDSET

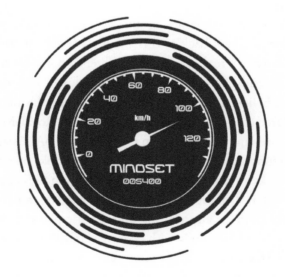

In my final year at school, I was the anchor for our house cross-country relay team. When I received the baton, I felt the overwhelming weight of responsibility to take the lead and finish strong. Instead, I mistimed my charge to the front of the field and ultimately failed in my mission. I crawled across the finish line and collapsed, unconscious.

I woke up with a drip in each arm and the suggestion that I should not participate in the individual event the following week. Thanks to the sanatorium support, I rehydrated sufficiently for a return to sports in a few days, but I was initially despondent about my chances in the individual event given the recent fainting incident.

I felt progressively stronger and more confident as it neared time for the individual run. On the day of the race, I got the strategy spot on and found myself in front with one kilometre to go. It was then a case of hanging on, crossing the finish line, and enjoying the sweet taste of victory.

When I look back at this small achievement from my school years, I realise it is a big reference point for how to overcome adversity, find the upside in a downturn, and help oneself believe that success can follow disappointment.

After school, I did eight years in the Royal Marines before moving to Cape Town to study an MBA. As an avid rugby supporter, I was excited to watch the Boks take on the All Blacks that year at Newlands. The evening before the Test match, I bumped into Joost van der Westhuizen. He had always been an inspiring and electric player to watch, and I'd listed him along with Nelson Mandela as a legendary South African I would love to meet in person.

Joost went on to play eighty-nine tests for the Boks. He led the team and led the most tries by a Bok for a long time, until Bryan Habana eventually overtook him. He was and always will be a hero of South African rugby.

In 2010, Joost was diagnosed with motor neurone disease. Instead of wallowing in self-pity, he faced this monster the same way he'd faced down Jonah Lomu in the 1995 RWC Final. He championed a foundation to raise money for research to help defeat this terrible disease.

Joost faced many setbacks in his life, but he never ever quit. I'm grateful I got to meet him, and I found his courage in the face of harrowing adversity to be one of the most inspiring reference points imaginable. He died aged forty-five and will be remembered for his indomitable warrior mindset, his unselfish fight for those who may suffer his fate with MND, and his dignity in death.

Reference points for inspiration need to be personal and meaningful. They give us role models, they help bring perspective, and they remind us that what has been done before, can be done again.

Inspiration

I love inspiring quotes and have come up with a few of my own over the years. It got me thinking. Which are the best quotes when it comes to building the right mindset? Which quotes pack a punch and make people want to roll up their sleeves and make a positive difference?

Of course, this is a subjective question, and different quotes will ignite different people for different reasons, but there are some quotes which have stood the test of time. Upon reflection, it did not surprise me to realise that these quotes are typically popular for three reasons: (1) an authentic and genuinely appealing message which feels intuitively true even if hard to achieve or believe sometimes; (2) a credible author with proven value to the world who "walked the talk"; and (3) the time that the quote was quoted—a general period or specific event which makes the message that much more poignant.

Michael Jordan's quote on the relationship between failure and success picks me up every time I am down.

> I've missed more than nine thousand shots in my career. I've lost almost three hundred games. Twenty-six times, I've been trusted to take the game winning shot and missed. I've failed over and over and over again in my life. And that is why I succeed.

Albert Einstein is famed for many quotes; this one reminds me to avoid the comfort zone.

> Anyone who has never made a mistake has never tried anything new.

Nelson Mandela is an icon for servant leadership. I treasure many quotes from him, but this one sums up the great man and reminds me to check my ego at the door and to lead the right way when I get a chance.

> It is better to lead from behind and to put others in front, especially when you celebrate team success. You take the front line when there is danger. Then people will appreciate your leadership.

Martin Luther King Jr brought together a divided nation through his courage, conviction, and faith. Amongst his many famous quotes, this one resonates enormously for me.

We must develop and maintain the capacity
to forgive. He who is devoid of the power to
forgive is devoid of the power to love. There
is some good in the worst of us and some
evil in the best of us. When we discover
this, we are less prone to hate our enemies.

Winston Churchill was a wartime leader who stood
at the abyss and galvanised the Allies in history's darkest
hour. His quote including the famous words "We will never
surrender" is legendary, but his simpler version is just as
powerful and applies on a daily basis.

Never, never, never give up.

Bringing it together for positive mindset, drawing on
the right quote at the right time can be a game changer.
There are also some quotes that have stood the test of time
and are certainly valuable for performance improvement.
Their messages make sense: Learning from failure leads to
success, the learning takes place outside the known comfort
zone, appropriate leadership is critical, forgiveness breaks
down barriers, and most important, never give up because
you are closer than you think to achieving the dream!

Finishing strong can be harder than it sounds. Our
natural human tendency is often to compromise our level
of excellence as time passes by. Standards can slip as we
experience performance creep, whereby best practice is
eroded, and poor practice becomes acceptable.

In sport, there are many examples of late comebacks
and corresponding flops. "Snatching defeat from the jaws

of victory" is a reference that no sportsperson or team wants to wear. Rather, "Snatching victory from the jaws of defeat" would be more aligned with finishing strong.

An example of a strong performance, but particularly a strong finish, which sticks in my mind from the Rio Olympics is the world-record-breaking 400-metre win by South Africa's Wayde van Niekerk. He was running in the outside lane and therefore had no visibility of the other finalists. He was always in the lead, but he needed a strong finish if he was going to eclipse the 43.18-second world record set by the legendary Michael Johnson in 1999. As he came around the final bend and into the home straight, it initially seemed that he was being caught by the two pre-race favourites. However, van Niekerk was merely shifting gears. In the final fifty metres, he accelerated away from the field and destroyed the world record to set a new mark of 43.03. His strong finish was pure inspiration, and he was named track athlete of the Rio Games.

Mo Farah is a GB favourite who also deserves mention for his incredible final laps to win the 5,000 metre race at both the London and Rio Games. Having won the 10,000 metres at both games as well, he is now one of very few Olympians to have won the "double-double".

There are hundreds of examples from dozens of sporting codes, of strong finishes which ignite the crowd and rewrite the history books. But finishing strong is a differentiator far beyond the world of sport.

Research has shown that in heavy industry projects and military campaigns, there is generally an increase in accidents and incidents towards the end. This is put down to human factors such as a loss of focus, a loss of leadership, and a compromised team approach as distractions and sometimes disillusionment or despondency creep in.

For this reason, it is vital that as a campaign winds down and the team is dissolved, a "best practice as usual" approach to performance, planning, and learning is led through to the very end. Not only that, but ideally a project retrospect should be held with all key stakeholders after project demobilisation to ensure that lessons are captured, discussed, and ultimately applied to future project management and for future benefit.

At a macro level as with the micro level, too often the emphasis is placed on a winning start rather than a winning finish. Proper pacing is essential to guarantee consistency throughout performance. We talk about safety, efficiency, and consistency; perhaps we should add legacy as a strong reminder that a campaign is not successfully complete until the final operation is safely done, the troops are home, and the project retrospect is facilitated, filed, and closed.

I recently finished an interesting book by Richard Reed called *If I Could Tell You Just* One *Thing*. It is effectively a transcript of the interviews that Reed conducted with dozens of famous people, and the focus is on each celebrity's best piece of advice to those seeking success in life.

Of course, the first point is that we need to be clear on our own definitions of success; that has a fundamental bearing on which advice will make most sense. Second, we probably have to accept that even with the same definition, advice that works for one may not work for another. That said, there were some interesting themes, and it got me thinking about what advice I might give my children.

My gut-feel top five are as follows.

1. Be yourself. Don't try to be someone else.
2. Do stuff you enjoy most of the time; this means that you need to find work that you enjoy too!
3. Don't beat yourself up if you make a mistake; learn what you need to and move forward. Also, forgive others who make mistakes; you know how it feels to mess up, so empathise and forgive, then provide support as necessary.
4. Show up; be present and prepared. "Anything worth doing is worth doing well."
5. Never give up—success could be just around the corner.

Good link

One way or another, this list is some of the best advice I have received and therefore the advice I would be happiest to impart.

Start with Why by Simon Sinek, is an inspiring and insightful book that I can thoroughly recommend. In his last chapter, Sinek offers a succinct summary of what distinguishes organizations that start with *why*.

Leadership

> We are continually improving at what we do, we come to work to inspire people to do the things that inspire them. If you believe what we believe and you believe that the things we do can help you, then yes, we are better than the competition. Our goal is to find customers who believe what we believe and work together so that we can all succeed, shoulder to

shoulder in pursuit of the same goals, not opposite each other in pursuit of a sweeter deal.

The concept of clients buying why you do what you do, rather than just what you do, is a paradigm shift that offers a healthy challenge to us all.

Apple is used as a strong reference point in Sinek's book due to the company's trail-breaking lead in challenging the status quo with all that they do. Sky's mantra is, "Believe in better." The Royal Marines ask if you have the necessary mindset or state of mind and believe that 99.9 per cent need not apply. It is the *why* aspiration that inspires interest, commitment, and loyalty from employees and customers alike.

If clients buy why we do what we do, it makes sense to take a moment to be very clear about our why.

As a performance coach, it certainly helped clarify my why: I have a personal belief that as individuals and within families and project teams, we are all capable of so much more than our current reality. As a company, Exceed believes that all project teams have strong potential for continuous improvement and innovation; this inspires me and completely aligns with my passion and aspiration.

The longest-running clients I have supported have been more like partners, and their belief rhymes perfectly with mine. They believe that their project teams can get better and better and that, as a collective, each team has huge potential to be world-class. Exceed brought the how and what expertise at a tactical level to support project leaders in catalysing the transformation, but the decision to involve us was based on our why: diverse and newly formed project teams have the potential within them to become world-class.

Sinek makes a point with which I agree: too many of us get stuck on promoting the how and what we do, which is important but not necessarily inspiring. It is certainly not conducive to long-term commitment.

Be clear about your why and inspire colleagues and clients who believe what you believe. The how and what will take care of themselves.

An excellent quote recently caught my eye. "Managers light a fire under you, leaders light a fire within you."

Les Brown, a US speaker and author, emphasises the importance of manifesting our dreams. He inspires, motivates, and persuades using personal anecdotes and professional learning to emphasise the following points.

1. It's possible (to achieve your dream).
2. It's necessary (to pursue your dream).
3. It's worth it (in the end, no matter the sacrifice, if you are being true to yourself and doing what you are passionate about, even if it is initially tough).

To create a spark, we need friction and traction; we need energy and synergy. When I was looking at my options beyond military life, I identified the MBA as an excellent catalyst for my professional journey, a way of harnessing my transferable skills and channelling them to create value in the commercial world. It was only when I took action to actually visit the business school in Cape Town and invest in the application process that my fire was fuelled, and there was no turning back.

Beyond business school, one of the tools which helped me crystallise my thinking about why and how I wanted to do what I wanted to do was the book *What Colour Is Your Parachute* by Richard Nelson Bolles. This book takes a structured approach to helping you figure out your future and emphasises the importance of pursuing what you are considered an expert at, as well as what you really enjoy doing; often those two answers coincide.

In *Good to Great* by Jim Collins, he talks about the hedgehog concept, which is three overlapping circles: What lights your fire (passion)? What could you be best in the world at (best at)? What makes you money (economic engine)?

Common to most respected guidance on the matter of creating value and achieving success is the key question of what you are passionate about, what you enjoy doing, and what lights your fire. If you can honestly figure that out and find work which allows you to express your passion, you are in the top 13 per cent of world workers, according to reputable Gallup surveys as referenced by Steve Crabtree in his 2013 article *Worldwide, 13% of Employees Are Engaged at Work*.

It is never too late to confirm what lights your fire, but don't leave it too late to ignite the flame.

Army Navy

A former Royal Navy rugby player and friend of mine, Chris, died when he was only fifty-two. His loss was a huge tragedy, and he was mourned by many who knew him for the standout gentleman that he was. One of the causes he was passionate about was the plight of service personnel with PTSD, and he'd been instrumental in the promotion of "The Mountain Way", which helps veterans with this condition.

Another friend of mine who also served and played with Chris is Kurt, an exceptional former Navy rugby player and former Marine. Kurt contacted me to explain that Chris had bequeathed some money in his will to be used by friends of his to celebrate his life at his most loved event, the Army–Navy game. It was an honour and privilege to be invited.

It was the hundredth British Army versus Royal Navy match at Twickenham, which in itself was special. It was also a sold-out stadium (eighty-five thousand people), which is incredible when you remember that in the 1990s, a crowd of twenty-five thousand for this match was a lot.

I met up with Kurt ahead of the Vets game in the morning, and we picked up the conversation where we'd left off when I'd last seen him twenty years ago. I reflected throughout the day on several truly inspiring elements of the experience.

1. The Camaraderie

The British Armed Forces are one big family, and this event certainly felt like one big reunion. Given the extent of military service and sacrifice particularly over the last twenty years since 9/11, it is a particularly poignant reunion. Many lives have been lost in combat, and many of those alive have scars on minds and bodies. For veterans of the brutal campaigns in Afghanistan and Iraq, as well as the ongoing war on terror, the Army–Navy game has become one of the major annual opportunities to reunite with comrades and to celebrate life and liberty.

I bumped into dozens of old friends with whom I'd served in the 1990s. We caught up and reminisced until we bumped into another old friend, and so it went on.

The network established while serving is equally key for business development; this reunion contributes to professional growth. My discussions with Kurt bore this out.

2. The Contest

Twickenham is a modern-day Colosseum befitting the gladiators who grace her glorious green pitch.

Eighty-five thousand spectators were treated to a magnificent contest involving forty-nine points in all, some superb tries, some bone-shaking tackles, and some breath-taking runs which brought the crowd to their feet and raised the roof with their roars.

I was very impressed by the quality of rugby on display, especially when you consider that these are serving personnel in a stretched British military. Getting consistency and continuity in this context must be a significant challenge.

There is also an accepted truth which is that the Army will generally start as favourites, but there is always the chance of an upset. The Navy statistically wins only once every six years nowadays, but as a former Marine and player myself, I believed the Navy could do it even when there was only a minute left on the clock!

In the end, the Army won 29-20, but the Navy played their hearts out, and I was proud of them. The contest was hard fought and played with guts, determination, dignity, and respect. The Army had some real X-factor players with lightning speed; they also converted their opportunities into points every time.

3. The Commitment

Player commitment was there for all to see, but what about spectator commitment? Armed Forces serving personnel and veterans had travelled from near and far to make the occasion. There were also thousands of civilian rugby fans and British patriots.

Beyond that, there was real commitment in terms of fancy dress. Whether a Corps coloured suit or impressive, authentic, "drag", supporters had gone to town.

Many conversations I joined were focused on finding ways to help those suffering from mental stress and PTSD. There was a real commitment to raise awareness and funds to mitigate and manage what has become a significant problem by many accounts. What was most humbling was that in some cases, the people collaborating to create a charity or join forces in the fight against PTSD were struggling themselves, but their focus was on helping those even less fortunate.

Prince Harry presided over the match as guest of honour, and indeed his Invictus initiative was the nominated charity for this year's event. This seemed entirely appropriate and continues the theme of "Help for Heroes". He was surrounded by some of the wounded Paralympic athletes who have inspired us all at the Invictus Games.

In conclusion, the day was a perfect match for Chris, whose life we celebrated. He was an incredible comrade to hundreds of people during his career. He played at Twickenham in the Army–Navy game and loved the contest and the challenge. His commitment on the field as a number 9 was a prelude to his subsequent commitment to values-driven leadership development and his passion for the "Mountain Way".

I left London inspired and humbled. There were so many heroes in one day. And what an amazing gesture from this servant leader, to bequeath a pot of money in his will for good friends who shared his passion for the Army–Navy game, to enjoy the occasion on his behalf. Goosebumps every time.

Springboks

The dust has settled, and we have had time to reflect on what the Springboks achieved in Japan at the 2019 Rugby World Cup.

I am an avid Springbok fan but also a passionate performance coach, so my reflections have drawn on the inspiration I felt during and after that final, as all the dots have joined up upon looking back.

I think the key difference between the two sides contesting the final was that it subsequently became clear the Boks were playing for something much, much bigger than a trophy. They had a purpose which transcended rugby; it was about uniting a troubled land and inspiring the next generation. Not only that, but key stakeholders within the squad have emerged from poverty to prove that anything is possible if you believe and put in the work.

When Rassie Erasmus was interviewed after accepting

best coach at the International Rugby Awards, he humbly cited three excellent points when asked how his team had won.

1. Belief. Belief in better, belief in each other, belief in what is possible. James Haskell summed it up perfectly in one of his vlogs: "Two years ago, South Africa couldn't win a raffle; now they have won the World Cup!" Rassie, Siya, and indeed the entire squad had to believe that despite some very poor results in 2017, "Big in Japan" could be done.

2. Luck. This is outside a team's control, so it is not a sound strategy to rely on luck. However, when it goes your way, your belief builds from possible to probable. New Zealand faced England in the first semi-final. It was an enormous game which did two things: it knocked out the defending champions, and it created unprecedented hype around the favoured England team. It was outside Bok control, but it was another stroke of luck for a team quietly on the rise.

3. Destiny. "Destiny is what is meant to be, what is written in the stars, your inescapable fate. There's no avoiding destiny—it's going to happen no matter what you do" (Vocabulary.com). One can't help feeling that the sequel to Invictus (Invictus II?) has now received its script, with the star being Siya Kolisi. The story could not be more inspiring: A black South African, born as Mandela was uniting a nation, learning to play rugby in a deprived area with little support. Against all odds, he went on

to captain the Springboks! It is the stuff of legend. Quite frankly, England did not stand a chance against this sense of destiny.

So, what can ordinary leaders and teams take from this extraordinary tale? In a word, inspiration. But we all know that before the inspiration comes a lot of perspiration. Belief grows when you are perspiring for a purpose which has real meaning (to all involved). Subordinate to that, of course, there needs to be exceptional talent and an outstanding training system, but history is littered with examples of wasted talent due to a lack of meaning or a weak sense of collective purpose.

The bottom line: you need buy-in, you need belief, and you need a sense of destiny.

Fosbury

Dick Fosbury came up with the "Fosbury Flop", clearing the bar backwards rather than forwards. It completely changed the way high jump was done, and it lifted performance over the next decade.

Between 1920 and 1968, the world record improved by fifteen centimetres. In the next ten years (after Fosbury flopped), it improved by the same height again! The Fosbury Flop became the standard.

Fosbury was called a genius once he won the Olympic gold medal in 1968, but prior to that achievement, very few people believed he was onto anything smart.

Fosbury wanted to raise the bar rather than raise his popularity with peers and coaches. He simplified his mindset to zoom in on exactly what the challenge involved, and then he took a fresh look at how that challenge could be overcome.

Mindset rather than skill set enabled the performance shift. Thinking inside the box was what all other high-jumpers at the time were doing; it was all about evolving the straddle-type clearance. Fosbury stepped back and considered the bigger picture, which at the time included the introduction of a softer landing mat. This led him to reset the problem and restart a solution.

He initially faced scepticism from the rest of the athletic world, but once he had won gold, the sceptics become supporters.

His mindset drove a new skill set which ultimately changed everyone else's mindset!

Servant Leadership

Nelson Mandela was a global inspiration, a national hero, and a true legend. In a world where many are losing faith in government, he was a beacon of hope. His story has understandably been told and retold in every form of media. His vision, his forgiveness, his sacrifice, his integrity, his commitment, his "belief in better", and his service to a nation, a continent, and a planet were unique.

He is one of the few irreplaceable mortal role models for servant leadership. Here are three simple points of association we can all use to become better servant leaders.

1. Be more like Mandela; read about him, listen to his speeches and interviews, look at photographs which illustrate his demeanour.
2. Earn respect rather than use rank or title. Respect is earned in the trenches, and in the board room, by doing what we say we will and by genuinely serving the team and the greater good.
3. Be a role model for others in terms of attitude and impact.

"Reach for the stars. You might not reach them, but at least you'll land on the moon." Mandela leadership is a super-stretch target, but modelling his aura, his approach to earning respect, and his character traits will drive all of us to better servant leadership.

I was lucky enough to speak at Leadercast Aberdeen. After my speaking part, I tuned into the speakers from the United States and noted some excellent observations which apply as much to personal leadership as to brand leadership. I reread my notes and was reminded of some of the valuable takeaways for individuals, coaches, and business teams.

1. Clarity—Is it absolutely crystal clear what we stand for and what we mean? A great way to lose credibility is to create confusion about our purpose. We should be associated with reliability and consistency rather than mixed messaging and double standards. Clear equals simple, simple equals memorable, and memorable is portable.
   Create a clear vision that people believe in.

2. Situational awareness—How do people experience you, and how do people experience themselves in your presence? This skill requires constant effort to improve, yet it is often paid mere lip service. Adjusting to different cultures and cues is a subtle art but is immensely significant in the context of our potential impact as leaders. Having created a clear vision, we now need to reinforce the behaviour that's aligned with that shared vision.

   Model consistently what we want to see in others.

3. Do the right thing—Focus on the right thing and impact everything. As leaders, we have an obligation to make things better even though things could be worse. In order to be the best we can be, as individuals or as teams, leadership requires decision-making, and this can separate good from great. It is the right way, rather than the easy way, that wins hearts, minds, and campaigns. Where needed, provide the skills to break new ground.

   We must keep ourselves and the team moving forward.

In summary, be crystal clear, be situationally aware, and always strive to do the right thing to keep moving forward.

There is a Gary Larson *The Far Side* picture which has stayed with me since the first time I saw it. It involves a man pushing hard on a door that clearly says "Pull". There is a simplicity about the individual, the picture, and indeed the message.

The applicable learnings for me are fourfold.

Be honest about shortcomings. I have been the guy in that Larson picture, pushing on a door which says pull. In fact, I think I have even had my hand on the word *pull* as I have been pushing before. I've also done the reverse and tried to pull on a door handle when the door says push. I accept that I do not always read the instructions when I should, and as a result, I occasionally slow myself down or repeat previous mistakes. More than that, sadly my ego and need to be right can often cloud good judgement, common sense, and smart decisions for the greater good.

Consider the bigger picture. There is a well-known saying: "Can't see the wood for the trees." This refers to our tendency to become so immersed in the doing and detail of a task that we do not maintain a big-picture perspective on what else is going on in the world and, indeed, which other doors may be open to us.

Pause before the push. Too often I have rushed into a challenge without pausing to consider my rationale for investing the time and energy, the potential consequences of said investment, and the opportunity cost of taking on this challenge. A pause helps to clarify the strategy as well as the tactical approach. In this case, pulling the handle to take the first step forward might be a more successful start.

Apply experiential learning. It is essential to find a way to continue the improvement journey, to continue learning (from others and ourselves), to find our callings, and to escape the pattern of repeated mistakes. There is no "one size fits all"; each individual or team has unique DNA. To this end, generic best practice needs to be tailored to a specific solution for success. Whatever the personal recipe, the proof will be in the pudding. Adapt accordingly.

Getting out of our own way is difficult, but it can be done. As a coach, I have noticed that these steps can help leaders and teams to open the door to better performance, acknowledge the gaps, consider options, pause to rehearse the chosen plan, and keep learning in order to improve for next time.

Growth Mindset

I enjoyed the book *Grit* by Angela Duckworth. Through extensive research and interviews with "Grit Paragons", as she describes them, the author spells out the power of passion and perseverance.

One of the themes which is reinforced throughout this valuable book is that of growth mindset. MINDSET describes a growth mindset thus:

> In a growth mindset, people believe that their most basic abilities can be developed through dedication and hard work—brains and talent are just the starting point. This view creates a love of learning and a resilience that is essential for great accomplishment. Virtually all great people have had these qualities. (mindsetonline.com)

MINDSET explains that the opposite of a growth mindset is a fixed mindset, whereby people believe that their basic qualities, like their intelligence or talent, are simply fixed traits. They spend their time documenting their intelligence or talent instead of developing them.

Growth mindset is the very essence of continuous improvement, and as a team performance coach, I truly believe that all competent teams can accomplish extraordinary results through passion and perseverance, provided they collaboratively and uncompromisingly commit to the necessary discipline of a deliberate performance-improvement process.

This belief is exemplified by the Seattle Seahawks' Super Bowl–winning football coach Pete Carroll and his coaching team, whose "grit culture" is described in Duckworth's book: "Always compete, be all you can be, strive together for excellence, finish strong."

I also remember a simple grit-truth from my training in the Royal Marines: "Train hard, fight easy."

At Exceed Performance, provided the correct and proven technology is in place, we believe that with committed leadership and the right approach to accelerated improvement, any competent team can achieve and sustain high performance.

The proven Exceed approach enables campaign leaders to build one team to achieve the collective mission: safe, compliant operations, with all objectives delivered, under budgeted time and cost.

Our process is simple but not necessarily easy—hence the need for strong leadership, implementation experience, and resilience. The focus needs to be on team unity, deliberate planning and learning, and recognition: Basically, it is a gritty growth mindset. With passion and perseverance, we can lead this proven team approach. Accomplishment will follow.

Coaching Approach

Many of us are familiar with the Tuckman team-growth curve. This model is accepted as a simple but accurate representation of the stages most teams pass through between formation and high performance.

Many of us are also familiar with the standard time and cost curves by which we track actual performance against planned performance in order to chart how operations are progressing on a project.

To beat normal progress and accelerate to high performance takes something extra. It takes innovation. It takes discipline. It takes leadership.

A proven element of the performance-coaching value proposition is the provision of expertise and experience to unleash the potential of a project team and to accelerate the normal team-growth curve by ensuring that agreed performance-improvement disciplines are uncompromisingly embedded and led from the get-go.

As Einstein said, "Insanity is doing the same thing over and over again and expecting different results." Innovation is now essential for high-performance acceleration; perhaps now is the time to consider accelerating project-team integration in order to stay ahead of the normal performance curve.

Performance Conscience

Conscience can be defined as a guide to behaviour.

The word *conscience* can be associated with knowledge, understanding, and doing the right thing.

In a frontline project team setting, I have often described the role of a performance coach as the team conscience because sharing knowledge, ensuring understanding, and doing the right thing is usually not the path of least resistance. However, just because it is not easy does not mean it is not right.

A simple but very effective analogy that most can relate to is personal fitness. Research has shown that nutrition is foundational for fitness. Yet despite this knowledge, many of us choose to compromise and eat junk.

It takes a little effort and planned time to eat well. We intuitively know that healthy food will lead to better health, but many of us decide that if we eat something (at some stage), we will still be fine.

A nutrition coach would strongly advise a healthy eating approach to set us up for a healthy day, a healthy month, and a healthy life.

Returning from the analogy, a great leader or coach appreciates the significance of marginal gains and the compound effect of doing the right thing over time. Smart eating each day is like a healthy planning meeting before each operation. Skipping the meeting or planning at random might not necessarily lead to trouble, but a proper planning meeting each time is more likely to lead to consistent success.

The refreshing value of an embedded performance coach is that the right conditions are created to make doing the right thing seem less like hard work! It would be like getting an alarm call at home and then arriving in the kitchen to find the right ingredients prepared for a healthy breakfast, thus leading to a healthy day. The right conditions are created for doing the right thing in order to give ourselves the best chance of success first time, every time.

A champion mindset, and the breakfast of champions, starts with a performance conscience.

Stay Hungry!

There is a well-known phenomenon whereby sports teams relax after just having scored, thus often allowing the opposition back into the game. The same can be said for business teams who have enjoyed a period of growth and then subconsciously slackened off through complacency and comfort.

Sustaining and maintaining performance at a high level is easier said than done. However, based on experience supporting dozens of high-profile frontline project teams, I'd reiterate that following these three very simple (but far from easy) habits can restore focus when distraction comes along.

1. Plan. Whether it is a planning meeting before an operational phase, or a regular huddle before key decisions are made, planning is crucial for unity and trust, as well as clarity and focus.
2. Review. Whether it is a sit-down discussion or a hot debrief post task, review allows for sharing and reflection in the moment, which triggers awareness.

3. Learn. Whether a conference call or a crew shift change, taking immediate action and rapidly applying lessons learned is a high-performance trait because it leads to quantifiable and positive change.

Top sports teams trigger renewed hunger in the heat of battle through an ongoing plan/review/learn cycle. Richie McCaw summed up this warrior mindset and general approach to maintaining focus on and off the field. In his movie *Chasing Great*, McCaw noted that every day, and after every score, he would "start again".

This trigger phrase reset the mind, the heart, and the hunger. Arguably the greatest rugby player ever, McCaw's approach may be worth modelling to combat complacency. The scoreboard is back to zero, the bank balance is back to zero, and the hunger is back to huge.

Undoubtedly the most significant leading indicator of team success is the ability to collectively and successfully transform in accordance to learning at the front line. This requires a well-led and hungry team, ready to give everything for the cause.

Like many, I have struggled with procrastination over the years. I have good intentions and set goals, but then I get distracted and delayed. Sound familiar?

Recently, I had something of an epiphany while listening to motivational speaker Eric Thomas. What he said is a simple truth but one which has helped me reframe the concept of procrastination.

Thomas mentions a woman who attended one of his seminars in Australia. She claimed to have a major problem with punctuality and procrastination, so he gave her this scenario: "If I offered you a million dollars to meet me at a certain location at 5 a.m., what would you do?"

She answered, "I'd be there at 4:59 no matter what!"

Thomas went on to confirm what we all intuitively know, which is that if something is important enough, we will prioritise it and will be on time. What each of us considers important may differ from one person to the next, but the principle remains the same.

Beating procrastination is about personal priority, reality, and honesty.

1. What is non-negotiable for you?
2. What is genuinely important to you?
3. What do you genuinely value?

Eric Thomas is known for popularising the quote, "When you want to succeed as bad as you want to breathe, then you'll be successful." It gets the point across. You must want something badly in order to beat procrastination. It is often people like Thomas who come from nothing and go on to achieve success: there was no fall-back option, and getting things done was non-negotiable.

If something is not important enough, it will be sacrificed or put off until another time. To avoid procrastination, we should set goals which align to what we genuinely believe we must achieve in order to survive and thrive. Then we need to be proactive, and we need to anticipate in order to stay ahead of deadlines and deliverables.

Everyone loves an underdog. The Rocky Balboa story appeals to everyone because we all face adversity at some time or another, and we seek inspiration to turn things around and triumph against the odds. All champions have had to fight through personal or public doubt. The few minutes of podium glory are built on years of sacrifice and hard work.

The Rocky film series was inspired by a real boxer, a relative unknown who went nearly fifteen rounds with the great Muhammad Ali.

Project teams are made up of many inexperienced and often unknown personnel. Teams are required to step into the proverbial ring and take on whatever challenges are thrown at them.

To become a champion team means that ordinary people need to achieve the extraordinary together. Many teams fail, just like many underdogs merely make up the numbers. So, what is the most important lesson we can learn from Rocky when it comes to reaching the top of the steps?

For me, the answer must be desire—a burning, inextinguishable desire to prove what is possible when you set your mind to it. Achieving collective desire in a new project team requires careful leadership and organisation. We call it "one team, one mission" and have an initial step in the Exceed approach which focuses on building team identity and inducting project members into the fold.

I'm reminded of one of my favourite quotes from Mark Twain: "It's not the size of the dog in the fight; it's the size of the fight in the dog." The underdog has the inextinguishable desire to fight through adversity and emerge unconquered at the top of the steps.

Exceed Expectations

As head of performance at Exceed, I have been privileged over the last thirteen years to support more than thirty-three project teams in the heavy industries, primarily oil and gas, and generally offshore.

As I reflect on those experiences, and indeed on what took the best of those campaigns to world-class performance, I always arrive at the same three key points. For simplicity I will use the three *L*s.

1.   Leadership.

It should not surprise anyone that when there has been strong, engaged, involved leadership, performance improvement has been extraordinary. There is a direct correlation.

Impactful leadership in this context looks like this: knowledgeable, visible, approachable, reliable, and sociable. A deficiency in any of those traits will detract from overall impact.

Most important is that the key leader needs to be around for the whole campaign, from start to finish. If continuity is lost at the top, performance will almost inevitably suffer.

2.   Lessons Learned.

The most important role we have as Exceed performance coaches at the front line is that of capturing all lessons on behalf of the team. Once captured, the lessons need to be addressed, progressed, understood, and then implemented so that next time the process is completed, the job is done more safely and more efficiently.

The best way to manage lesson closure is to have regular (weekly) "close-out calls" between the front-line leadership team and the head office leadership team.

On campaigns where this discipline has been maintained throughout, the performance improvement has been extraordinary. There is a direct correlation.

3.   Let the process work!

Although we do not lay claim to a silver bullet, we have learned a thing or two about how to build teams, accelerate the learning curve, and help leaders achieve objectives and deliver results. At Exceed Performance, it is our value proposition. It is what we do.

It can therefore be somewhat frustrating when prospective clients prescribe the approach they would like for their own performance improvement while asking us to help. It is a bit like going to a back specialist, asking for help to fix our back pain, but telling the specialist how to do the fix.

Our leading indicators for improvement have evolved through more than a decade of feedback and experience as specialists in this service. The process works. Give it a chance.

In this age of instant gratification, we often encounter teams seeking a silver bullet—a culture transformation overnight. It does not exist.

The process takes time and requires investment. The steps are simple but not easy. However, if the process is sponsored with courage and commitment, the return is world-class performance. There is a direct correlation.

The three *L*s lead directly to the three *M*s: Leadership drives team mindset, a learning approach is the most proven method, and letting leadership and team learning unlock excellence is the best mood to maintain.

Mindset over Skill Set

Selecting and training performance coaches is a privilege that I will never take for granted. We are always on the lookout for servant leaders who have the right mindset to learn the skill set and embrace the unique challenges associated with an influencing role in high-cost, high-risk, high-ego environments.

The course allows attendees to decide whether the performance coach role is for them while also allowing the course facilitators to gauge who has what it takes to make the transition from a previous position to that of a performance coach.

From a big-picture perspective, the aim is to help the prospective coaches experience accelerated team bonding, accelerated learning, and inspiring leadership in a safe environment so that they have a reference point for what they will be expected to deliver on behalf of the teams they are fortunate enough to support.

At a personal level, the aim is to introduce the prospective coaches to the tools of performance improvement so that they commence or increase their competence and confidence with skills they may not have had to develop in former roles.

Feedback I have had from previous students regarding

what inspires and excites them about the coach training course points to the learning of new skills such as video editing, or the positive disruption of their frame of reference for something they may have touched on before such as leadership or presentation skills.

If sessions such as these are instructed by credible experts and facilitated in a fun, dynamic way, the participants feel they are receiving transferable value, and their appetite for some of the more mundane aspects of the course will increase.

Ultimately, there needs to be engagement and a sense of personal enhancement for people on a training course to truly achieve enjoyment. Interaction with interesting individuals and informative insights can lead to inspiration and a sense of valuable growth or "time well spent". I personally love facilitating the performance coach training courses because I learn from each and every course member throughout the week. Immersion in the process inspires me every time!

Mental Toughness

Different examples come to mind for different people when you hear the phrase "mental toughness". One thing is for sure: the influence our minds have on our performances cannot be underestimated.

A great mental toughness analogy I have heard relates to a car dashboard fuel gauge. The body wants to stop working when the indicator reaches the red line; the mind, however, knows that there is another 10 per cent left in the tank. If our minds are strong enough to keep our bodies going, it is a 10 per cent competitive advantage!

Mental toughness is also about keeping an ice-cool head during the intense heat of battle. One of my mentors, Steve Harris, used to talk about fire and ice, and he developed a structured approach to building mentally tough rugby players when he and I were working with the future stars of South African rugby. Together, we created workshops and breakaways for professional teams, which integrated mental-toughness theory with practical challenges to illustrate and manifest the benefit of enhanced mental skills.

In my own experience as a Commando captain, CrossFitter, and coach, there are four trigger statements which best exemplify mental toughness for me.

1. Expect the unexpected. As a marine, this was a phrase with which I became well acquainted. It becomes a mindset. By subconsciously planning for the worst, it is always a bonus if the worst does not occur. An outcome different to what was expected, if not the worst possible outcome (someone died), is still not as bad as it could have been and is therefore a bonus! Improvise, adapt, and overcome is what commandos are taught. The circumstances have changed, it was unexpected, but we need to crack on. Embrace this attitude, and we'll be on our way to mentally tough.

2. Finish strong. This became my rallying cry as a leader of teams in sports as wide-ranging as rugby and adventure racing. I now apply it on projects with our coaching teams. The temptation is for our

effort level to drop as we approach the end of a challenge. It is all too easy to coast to the finish line, especially if those around us are doing the same. But if we make it a habit to accelerate rather than brake around the final bend, it will become second nature and will override the quit button when the going gets really tough.

3. Compete every time. I got into CrossFit in 2012. At a stage when I was finding the gym somewhat monotonous, it was exactly what I needed, and I have never looked back. That said, high-intensity workouts are not for the faint of heart, and the few competitions I have attended can brutally expose poor technique or a weak engine if you are not fully prepared. This year, I decided to make a step change mentally; I treat every training workout as if it is a competition, and as a result, I am less and less intimidated by competition or new exercise combinations. It becomes business as usual no matter how big the stage. Physically I am getting fitter, but mentally I am tougher as well.

4. Focus on process. This point has been reiterated to me a few times in recent autobiographies and articles I have read. If you attach success to outcomes and you fail to achieve these, you feel like a failure. If you attach success to process, you build confidence provided you commit. The process is completely owned by us and is not subject to forces outside our control (which is the case with outcomes). However, if the process or training program has been carefully designed to achieve the best possible

improvement, the outcomes will follow. Confidence is a key mental skill, so an increase in this means a tougher mind overall.

In each of the four areas, rebounding from failure and maintaining resilience in adversity has been key. Never give up. This is important in the context of individual and team performance, where setbacks can seem terminal. Yet once overcome, they are simply lessons learned.

Expect the unexpected, always finish strong, train hard, and focus on the process. This combination has enabled me to face down a few giants in my time.

Olympics

Every four years, we are reminded of what is humanly possible. We are inspired by feats of heroism and athleticism that transcend the extraordinary. But the most amazing aspect of this sporting spectacle is that for the most part, these feats are achieved by "ordinary-looking" people.

If you lined up ten amateur sportsmen, you couldn't necessarily pick out the Olympian simply by physical appearance. Of course, this applies to some sports more than others, but the point is made: It is what you don't see that has the biggest impact on performance, even at the Olympic level!

We are talking about positive mindset—commitment, discipline, self-belief, and determination. This can turn ordinary into extraordinary; in skilled athletes and Olympic teams with visionary leadership and world-class coaching, this turns to gold.

Champion project teams can learn from this. Assembling the right people with the right skills is essential, and strong leadership is key, but inspiring the Olympic mindset will get us over the line in record time.

The Paralympics promotes this point to a whole new level. Impossible is nothing, as they say.

What can we learn from the Olympics? Probably a number of lessons, but the most obvious to me is this: We are all capable of so much more.

Kipchoge

We live in extraordinary sporting times. Not only have we seen a bolt from the Caribbean blue who destroyed sprint records in the last decade, but we have recently witnessed marathon magic too!

Eliud Kipchoge ran 1:59:40 to achieve the seemingly impossible: 26.2 miles under two hours.

He achieved this in special conditions in Vienna where the course and the Ineos-sponsored pacing team were designed to enable best possible performance. But ultimately, he still needed to show up and maintain a pace of 4:34 per mile—yes, four-and-a-half-minute miles—for 26.2 miles!

Roger Bannister did the first mile under four minutes in 1954—another seemingly impossible feat at the time.

Kipchoge had made one earlier attempt at the two-hour barrier in 2017. This one was organised by Nike in Italy. It was called "Breaking 2", but he finished just outside the two-hour mark on that occasion.

What I find very interesting is the psychology involved. The first run was focused on the two, and it seems that for a long time, Kipchoge was running around the two-hour mark. Then finally Ineos decided to focus on 1:59, and guess what? Kipchoge ran 1:59.

When Bannister finally broke four minutes for a mile and ran 3:59.4, many others broke the four-minute barrier within a matter of months. What we believe and target, we manifest. It is as simple as that.

Kipchoge was recently a guest at the Aberdeen-hosted BBC sports personality of the year award. The point he made during his speech was that human potential is unlimited. He has proven wrong all the forecasters who said that a sub-two-hour marathon would likely be many decades from now. The same was said to Bolt about his time for the 100m sprint.

What is our 1:59? Be specific and target exactly what you want, no matter how "impossible" someone tells you it is. Our human potential should not be limited by our mindset. Rather, it should be unlocked by belief and action.

Shark

I have recently enjoyed listening to Walter Bond on YouTube. He talks about a shark mindset: keep moving forward, don't stop, and own your destiny. He talks about the phenomenal mentoring influence of his father and the point at which he went from "sucker fish" to "shark" by seizing the opportunity to be true to himself and to follow his truth, his purpose, and his dream.

Bond always wanted to play for the NBA, but a series of injuries and increasing self-doubt led him to the brink of surrender. Then his father reminded him of his ambition when he was younger: to play professional basketball. Accountability, integrity, and delivering on your word were the only currencies in the Bond family home. It was a matter of honour to follow through on your purpose and on what was possible, even if it was highly improbable.

An optimal mindset unlocks potential, which takes impossible to "I'm possible". A big-picture example is the landing of a man on the moon. In 1960, many said this was impossible to achieve. However, John F. Kennedy altered this international mindset with his impassioned speech in 1961 when he expressed his vision of a man on the moon by the end of the decade. Apollo 11 and Neil Armstrong accomplished the "impossible" moon landing in 1969.

Nelson Mandela said, "It always seems impossible until it is done." He should know—he helped his divided country to become a rainbow nation while also inspiring the Springboks to an extremely improbable Rugby World Cup victory over the All Blacks in 1995!

With a shark mindset, the moon is reachable, records can be broken, and the impossible can be done. The only question is whether we believe, and whether we are prepared to keep moving forward, no matter what stands in our way.

Mindset Accelerators

1. Practice servant leadership
2. Develop a growth mindset.
3. Find work that you enjoy.
4. Show up. "Anything worth doing is worth doing well."

5. Create a clear vision in which you and your team believe. Focus to manifest it.
6. Be yourself. Don't try to be someone else.
7. Earn respect by doing what you say you will. Serve the team.
8. Be an optimist.
9. Model consistently what you want to see in others.
10. Be honest about your shortcomings.
11. Consider the bigger picture. Serve the greater good.
12. Identify reference points for inspiration that are personal and meaningful.
13. Be clear about your "why" and inspire others who believe what you believe.
14. Apply experiential learning.
15. Forgive others; it breaks down barriers.
16. Car dashboard fuel gauge: 10 per cent still in the tank at "empty".
17. Kennedy: Man on the moon.
18. Kipchoge and Bannister: Run through the perceived barrier.
19. Mandela: "It always seems impossible until it is done."
20. Lincoln: Never give up; success could be around the corner.

DIAL 2

METHOD

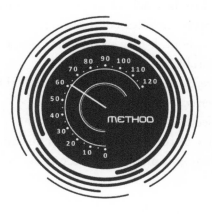

One significant observation after the 2016 UK and US elections was the outright refusal by many to accept the results of the democratic voting process. Further, it appeared that many key leaders had not truly kept in touch with reality.

Understandably, many people were frustrated and genuinely concerned about the future when the results were announced. But I want to focus on the disbelief and disdain; the leaders who refused to accept that their campaign assumptions could be incorrect.

Their "feedback denial" reminded me that in general, we tend to have a reluctance to believe or accept feedback if it does not align with our perception of reality.

I have seen this phenomenon play itself out on project operations, and it can negatively affect safety, welfare, efficiency, and profit. It is often explained as a form of cognitive bias or a tendency to think in a way that deviates from rationality and good judgement.

For example, when performance is worse than expected on a deliverable, we as leaders can make assumptions about why the performance was suboptimal. Worst case, we can become deaf to the feedback from those involved; feedback which probably includes contributing factors we do not want to hear about. It may even include the fact that we are part of the problem.

The spread of the Corona Virus COVID-19 in early 2020 is a perfect example of this.

2016 elections and the 2020 pandemic remind us of the criticality of these components for sustained recovery, continued improvement, and indeed realisation of full potential.

1. Servant leaders.
2. Committed team.
3. Proven process.
4. Frank communication.

Servant leaders listen to the team and serve the team, not the other way around. A committed team takes extreme ownership and gets the job done.

A proven process includes listening to the views of

experienced people and respecting the feedback. It includes planning and learning, analysing and recognising. It relies on frank communication which will only exist if the culture encourages that.

As with elections and pandemics, feedback is fundamental to progress. Identified issues must be addressed, lessons must be learned, and the team must be heard. Leaders who ignore these points will one day lose the vote.

Front Line Leadership

I like to provide insights from the front line about leadership and performance, learning, and methods that achieve results. Often my observations uncover subtle habits and behaviours which have a big impact on teamwork and morale.

The leader in this case now supervises drilling operations on a rig offshore. With significant technical experience, he attended a performance coaching course I ran many years ago. It was obvious then that he is a naturally curious and determined individual. He wanted to expand his skill set and evolve his mindset.

Fast-forward to the present, and I had the privilege of returning to the front line to support his operation.

Despite constant setbacks and an ongoing period of troubleshooting, I was extremely impressed by the way he conducted himself and how he led the offshore team. Below are ten habits that I noticed about this impressive front-line leader. They are simple habits; however, they are not often seen together, and they do enable a true "one team" spirit.

1. Take your job seriously but not yourself. Be humble and self-deprecating. Make jokes at your own expense on occasion. Have no ego.

2. Make time for everyone, no matter how busy. Have an open door at all times. Have no hidden agenda. Get back to people if you say you will. Respond to emails which are adding value to the campaign.

3. Take time to recognise team members who help the operation progress. Have no exceptions and no favourites. Give consistent recognition of those who deserve praise for going the extra mile, no matter the wider context.

4. Take ownership and defend the team when needed. Have a "no blame" culture. Say what needs to be said and stand up for the team when appropriate.

5. Do the right thing. Support the agreed process for planning and learning. When there is not time for an agreed meeting, apologise and look for a win-win compromise.

6. Be sure to know what is going on. Take time to read relevant information to be informed about the technology and interfaces involved. Ask questions and be curious. Listen to the answers.

7. Have grace under pressure. Follow the swan analogy: when things have gone wrong, remain calm and unruffled on the surface while the legs are paddling furiously out of sight. Pause and count to ten before reacting to unwelcome news. Seek to understand.

8. Give everyone a voice in meetings. Allow people to be heard.

9. Be human. Accept that you make mistakes. Ask for advice if you feel someone else might be able to help.
10. Delegate in such a way that team members look forward to doing the task for you.

These leading leadership indicators impact key lagging indicators. In close-knit frontline communities, one of these outcomes is the level of respect and collaboration displayed by the regular crew. This was clearly evident, and it was remarked upon by all who visited.

> "Leadership is practised not so much in words as in attitude and actions." —Harold Geneen

Continuity

We cannot underestimate the significance and importance of leadership continuity.

Sports teams that undergo wholesale changes to the leadership group tend to struggle, whereas teams with leader continuity and long-range succession plans tend to succeed.

In a Forbes leadership article, Don Yaeger wrote the following: "Over the years I've spent studying team dynamics, I've learned that the single greatest predictor of sustained excellence is continuity at the top. If you are a fan of the New England Patriots, you know that the consistent leadership at the helm of your favourite team has much to do with why you're annually relevant."

He goes on to say, "Yet we rarely allow leaders time to truly establish the culture that will allow their team to win … The truth is, building a team and creating a culture takes time and patience."

The All Blacks are surely another great example of leadership continuity, and reassuringly enough, their results are second to none.

Continuity, as a contributing factor to high performance, cannot be underplayed. It is a critical success factor and should be treated as such.

Expectancy

Whatever you focus on, expands. There is a large body of research around the concept and value of goal setting and visualisation. In my experience, there is no doubt that aiming at a clear target increases the likelihood of hitting it or at least getting closer than if there was no aim or no target at all.

There is a well-known quote about measuring to manage: "If you don't measure, you can't manage." To this end, we establish (daily updated) performance boards and a weekly performance slide on all project installations so that the team's performance against agreed metrics and targets is visible and current. Whether good news or bad news, everyone is in the loop.

Standard metrics include HSE events, achievement of set objectives, cost, total time, and productive time percentage. Not only are these boards and slides visible, but they are also regularly referenced and explained at weekly meetings and in monthly newsletters so that all personnel can become familiar with the numbers and charts.

I was on another project where the performance

illustration was even simpler. We had a poster of a barometer, and the 100 per cent mark on this represented the stretch target for the financial year. Progress was then updated on a weekly basis such that every member of the team could see the progress relative to the target. The barometer was in a highly visible area of the workplace to ensure focus and awareness.

In order to make performance personal, there needs to be a strong connection between leadership and the workforce. Progress needs to be well communicated, clear, and current. Ideally, team members need to be able to see how their specific actions contribute to project performance progress.

The bottom line: ensure every stakeholder on the project team is given the best possible chance to focus on performance targets and indicators, and we you expand the likelihood of project success.

Preparation

Project teams often wrestle with the question of whether they should manage important workshops internally, or whether they should outsource the facilitation to an external provider.

Having made the decision to invest in external expertise, it is interesting to note the attendant team's feedback on the benefits of their investment. Below is a list of the main points they made.

1. Given the workloads currently faced by key stakeholders, it meant that they did not need to

worry about preparation for the workshop, or indeed tracker population and report compilation post workshop. That is all taken care of.

2. Not having to manage the participation and contribution during the sessions enabled the workshop sponsors to fully participate and contribute themselves, without worrying about anything else.

3. The external facilitator is unaffected by historical political dynamics within the assembled team. He or she can be completely objective throughout.

4. A good facilitator thinks outside the box and innovates a bespoke approach to the gathering based on the specific workshop objectives. The workshop agenda is co-shaped to guarantee leadership enrolment, but a world-class facilitator is obliged to challenge what has been done before and suggest new ways to add value. This was very much the case here as we rolled out a novel "physical visual" way to highlight risks and key focal points.

5. Their final observation was that excellent facilitation is a skill which is developed like any other skill over many years and many workshops. The cost of all attendees' time for a day away from other operational responsibilities is significant. Surely it makes sense to get maximum return on that time and cost by using someone with the proven skill set to help achieve just that?

Value versus cost should be the clear winner if you have found a quality facilitator for your workshop.

There is always value in requesting feedback from the client sponsor of a workshop. In this case, we facilitated a planning and risk assessment session in Aberdeen to ensure no stone was left unturned in readiness for the client's forthcoming abandonment campaign.

The feedback reinforced many of the known benefits of outsourcing workshop preparation, facilitation, and post-workshop transcription to a team of professionals who specialise in accelerated project performance improvement.

1. Event organisation: The client should be protected from any time-consuming administration given their busy operational focus.

2. Stake holder representation: Significant effort should be made to ensure that all specialists are in attendance and that front-line personnel are there in number.

3. Time value maximization: Set the best possible agenda to achieve the workshop objectives and then ensure that a fine balance is maintained between delivering to deadlines and being flexible when certain issues need to be further explored, often in deliberate focus groups.

4. Setting the standard: The professionalism, team interaction, and intellectual rigour evidenced at the workshop establish the expectation for the project. In other words, start as you mean to for the campaign to go on.

5. Accurate record keeping: It is crucial that issues, actions, risks, and programme improvements are accurately and comprehensively spelled out and

subsequently captured for further examination and resolution.

Of course, as with all things, there will be room for improvement after every workshop. In this case, we identified an opportunity to be smarter in our organisation of the groups for the discussion sessions, as well as in our prioritization of key issues requiring special focus teams. A wash-up of the first major project evolution also sets the right precedent for all operations to follow.

Finally, optional initiatives such as a comprehensive project workshop, require strong and visionary leadership to take place at all—another reminder that high performance starts with exceptional project leadership.

I had the privilege of facilitating a management team breakaway for a company in the nuclear sector. The team was interested in a transferable improvement approach from other industries including the military and oil and gas.

We shaped an agenda which focused on building a stronger team on day one and a stronger forward strategy on day two. As with all good workshops, we kept it dynamic, interactive, and slightly outside the comfort zone such that true learning and outside-the-box thinking was essential.

Using the Gallup Strengths Finder reports for each team member's top five strengths, we created the space and time for people to explain their respective strengths and whether they felt their current roles made the most of these strengths. Group feedback to every individual promoted further awareness and ensured that constructive dialogue evolved regarding business value and using the right people for the right tasks based on their strengths profile.

Envisaging a desired future which addresses the rapidly changing market landscape required creativity and clarity, especially when the teams only had three hours to convert their ideas into a three-minute movie. Engagement was excellent, and the exercise served as a bridge between strength and strategy.

Day two dove further into the steps required to get from current reality to desired future, but it also drew on learnings from performance improvement in the oil and gas industry, which has faced similar challenges in terms of cost efficiency and risk management. Teams worked hard to identify clear aspirations and concrete actions to mitigate market forces, and finally each person recorded a measurable commitment to the team for 2017.

A strong strategy is key for survival, and a strong team knows the strengths of its members. Focusing on what we do have and what we can do has a compound effect on confidence and resilience in the face of uncertainty and change. I learned a lot facilitating the process, and witnessing renewed team cohesion was as humbling as ever.

Teamwork

Royal Marines

Benchmarking the best is always good practice. When it comes to high-performance teams, we don't need to look far beyond the British Commandos. In fact, it was for this very reason that the England Rugby Team sought help from the Corps ahead of their World Cup–winning campaign in 2003.

What are key elements of Royal Marines' teamwork? What can project teams take away from the elite in order to gain a competitive advantage at the front line?

1. It is a state of mind: From the outset, the Royal Marines are looking for attitude rather than aptitude. It is the former that will get you through the tough times, together. We have a quote on the wall here: "Tough times don't last; tough people do."

2. Serving something bigger than each individual: The project identity, legacy, and traditions need to unify all team members such that no one person ever becomes bigger than the team or the mission.

3. Core values: The Royal Marines' values are excellence, integrity, self-discipline, and humility. Simple explanations are attached to each so that all marines know how to apply these values to daily tasks. The values are tangible.

4. Commando spirit: They have courage, determination, unselfishness, and cheerfulness. Spirit is the X factor, the ethos. It is the non-physical part of a person which is the seat of emotions and character—the soul. Marines aspire to embody these characteristics.

5. Personal and professional development: Royal Marines do not sit still. They are always trying to improve themselves, learn new skills, achieve the next level of capability, and influence in order to be

better assets to the team. Each marine and team is trying to be the best they can be.

In summary, the Royal Marines can teach us a huge amount about world-class teamwork. Fundamental to their high performance is a positive mindset, willingly serving the cause, tangible values, Commando characteristics, and a tireless pursuit of personal and professional growth.

I was privileged to be part of this extraordinary organisation for eight years. It was an honour to serve, and what I learned about high-performance teams has been invaluable ever since.

All Blacks

In the context of performance, we cannot ignore the most successful sports team of all time. The All Blacks have a win rate of 78 per cent but are at 84 per cent since the game went professional and over 90 per cent since 2010!

There are as many reasons why other countries should be better than New Zealand as there are superlatives to describe the class of their rugby. Yet they continue to dominate in a way which very few other teams of any type can emulate.

The book *Legacy* by James Kerr explores and unpacks fifteen themes which differentiate the All Blacks and provide lessons in leadership for anyone willing to learn. It is one of the best books I have ever read.

I will go with my gut on the three most aspirational and transformational components of the All Black legacy from a high-performance perspective. Here are three boosters for an unstoppable force.

1. Haka. All rugby followers enjoy watching the haka before a test match. The Maori battlefield war cry is fixating, and for All Black opposition, it must be hugely intimidating. But more than that, I think what project teams can take from the traditional haka is the significance of the investment made in a ritual which has nothing to do with the specific technical skills required to win the rugby match.

    There is no doubt that the haka gives the All Blacks a competitive advantage despite not involving a rugby ball, a pass, a kick, or a tackle. The haka clearly enables incredible intangible integrity; it builds up the team to be truly greater than the sum of its parts. It inspires collective self-belief, fearlessness, and camaraderie. It is about identity, unity, history, and legacy.

2. Continuity. Succession planning in the All Blacks has become world-class since the beginning of the professional era. There seems to be an instinctive mentorship programme whereby older players and former players fiercely protect the All Black brand and ensure that younger players entering the fray are inducted into this vital mindset. Players are required to leave the jersey in a better place than when they received it.

    For project teams, the aspiration is surely to inspire experienced campaigners to mentor and model the requisite approach to achieve the best possible results so that younger team members understand and revere the expectation from the get-go.

3. Stamina. A signature of many All Blacks victories is the scoring of points late in the game to secure the win. They have a renowned "finish strong" mentality. There are games where the All Blacks have displayed remarkable composure and concentration to string upwards of twenty phases together before crossing the chalk for an injury-time try. The point is that they clearly train stamina as a genuine competitive edge. When other teams are tiring or quitting, the All Blacks are shifting into top gear. They are instinctively accelerating to another level.

If project teams can use relevant training and experience to promote team stamina, they too can go the extra mile as standard in order to win more and fulfil latent potential.

In summary, the All Blacks clearly epitomise high performance, so it is worth studying them and adopting transferable elements to improve project teams. They unleash true potential through a unique identity which is held in the highest regard and passed on from one generation to the next. They also have a specific focus on stamina to finish stronger than all the competition and to get the job done.

I'm a diehard green-and-gold Springbok supporter, but there is no doubt the benchmark is All Black.

Family

Like many people, I have been involved in team building for a long time. It started at school, learning how to get the best out of our boarding house, track relay, and rugby teams. Then it continued in the marines, learning how to unite warriors behind a mission; in the corporate world as a workshop facilitator; and finally, in the oil industry, striving for the secret to team success as both a project manager and performance coach.

I have been searching for the key ingredients of a high-performing team, and though I will not claim to have found the perfect recipe, I will say that by reflecting on one other (much more significant) learning experience, I feel a breakthrough coming on. I'm talking about family!

As a child and sibling, while growing up, I had some appreciation of teamwork to get things done. As a co-parent of three young kids, I now have a crystal-clear insight into the difference between average and amazing family work. In a genetic family environment, when all family members discuss and truly collaborate to successfully implement a plan, the sense of satisfaction is immense. When this family teamwork performs under pressure against a threatening challenge, the bond becomes primal.

Maybe this is why elite professionals who are part of world-class teams talk about their communities as family. It is effectively the highest honour that can be given to a generic team—brothers in arms, band of brothers, blood family.

If we accept that special team communities aspire to become a family, we need to explore what makes a special family. In theory, if we understand this, we may have the key to unlocking world-class teamwork. We'll focus here on five key contributing steps to becoming a super family.

1. Sacrifice. This speaks for itself, and in one word, it provides a perfect anchor for family actualisation. Parents and children in any functioning family

understand that there is more than just themselves to think about. This means compromising on the personal wish list and involves serving other family members to maintain overall progress.

2. Support. The stronger the mutual support in the family, the greater the chances of family security and future growth. Being there for each other, and particularly parents being there for their children, is the foundation of trust, loyalty, and integrity.

3. Stability. A confident family unit is built on a stable platform, an island of calm even when the surrounding seas might be somewhat rough. This requires reliable, accountable family members and a familiar home base. It enables identity.

4. Systems. Spontaneity is important, but there must be a fundamental set of guidelines and principles from which the family operates. This provides structure. Routines and checklists are generally followed as standard.

5. Success. This can be measured in many ways, but it is vital for morale and for momentum. Celebrating success is central to a happy family, and members are motivated to achieve more based on how they see success benefiting the family unit.

World-class teamwork is indeed a lofty goal. It continues to be the focus for millions of people and billions of dollars. There are thousands of books on the subject. Potentially it is naïve to try to simplify the concept, but I am certain that top teams talk about being a family, and family undoubtedly benefits from the five Ss listed above.

Reunions and relationships forged during tough team campaigns bear out the link. Going from team formation to family status can be a very long journey, but the steps above at least provide a start.

Natural World

Instinct is an innate, typically fixed pattern of behaviour in animals in response to certain stimuli. If we turn to the natural world, we can find some truly inspiring teamwork borne of survival instinct and experiential learning. If nothing else, these well-researched behavioural patterns provide food for thought and promote wonderful admiration.

We'll consider three examples: one from the sea, one from land, and one from the air. We'll identify a striking idiosyncrasy for each and then pull it all together.

A pod of dolphins will circle and herd a school of fish into a tightly packed "bait ball" and, if possible, even guide the fish into shallow water. Once there, the dolphins take turns ploughing through the bait ball, gorging on the fish as they pass through. Scientists have observed that dolphins have such control of this method that it is almost impossible for the fish to escape until each dolphin has had its fill. Working as a team, the dolphins are much more successful than if they worked alone.

A pack of wolves has a consistent order of march when moving from point A to B. The three wolves at the front are the sick and elderly; they are sacrificial in the event of an ambush. Equally, their pace sets the tempo for the rest of the pack so that they do not get left behind. They are followed by the five toughest young wolves, then the rest of the pack, followed by another five tough wolves towards the rear. Trailing behind is the alpha wolf, surveying it all and maintaining strategic control. Each wolf does what is best for the pack. This approach applies to their every endeavour.

A flock of geese flies in a *V* formation so that each goose provides additional lift and reduced air resistance for the goose flying behind. By flying together in a *V* formation, scientists estimate that the whole flock can fly 70 per cent farther with the same amount of energy than if each goose flew alone. The geese rotate positions to share the load, and they have learned that this team approach is the smart way to travel.

Many of us have come across these phenomena, and the transferable lessons are nothing new. However, a reminder and a mental picture, along with a description of the key facts, can restore our aspiration to emulate Mother Nature.

1. Individual success often relies on well-coordinated teamwork.
2. Extreme ownership of our team role ensures the team survives to succeed.
3. Smart organisation and collaborative effort help the team go even further together.

I have always been instinctively inspired by excellent teamwork; these truths from the wild are worth noting for acceleration to automatic achievement.

Keep It Simple

Keep it simple, stupid. The acronym KISS is one with which many of us are familiar because it has been around for a long time. But it seems more relevant now than ever before.

In recent times, I have heard many colleagues and clients stress the importance of keeping t simple. It reminds me of the quote by Albert Einstein: "The definition of genius is taking the complex and making it simple." It is certainly relevant in today's world of information overload.

Although simple does not necessarily mean easy, we are dead in the water if we can't even communicate a message.

To this end, I will apply KISS and note three suggestions to simplify life from the audiobook *Peak Performance* by Brad Stulberg and Steve Magness.

1. Routine. Successful people stick to the same routine when it comes to preparation and readiness to execute. It is familiar and therefore allows focus and composure.
2. Timing. Successful people identify their optimal time for productivity. For some, it is early in the morning; for others, it is late at night. Most important, your chosen productive time needs to be best for you.
3. Surroundings. Successful people understand the importance of creating the correct surroundings and conditions for high performance. Like routine and timing, it is not left to chance.

In summary, simple is essential for optimal performance, and for a greater chance of success. Routines, times, and surroundings are mostly within our control to optimise for us and for our teams.

Let's turn KISS into "Keep it Simple, Smart"!

Paint a Picture

Imagery is powerful. One of my favourite metaphors is the elephant in the room.

I find myself constantly searching for analogies to help naysayers understand the value of coaching. One of my favourites is the GPS and map analogy: We can plug a post code into a GPS and follow instructions to get us to a destination. That is fine; we do it often. But if there comes a time when there is either no address or no GPS, and we have not invested time in understanding how to read a map, we will be lost. Coaches help us learn to navigate our own way rather than relying on someone else for the answer. This builds internal capacity. It generates self-improvement. It unleashes latent potential. In short, coaching enables individuals and teams to drive better results for themselves – this is reinforced by commentary from uber-successful entrepreneurs like Bill Gates.

One of the oldest but best performance-coaching analogies I have come across is the comparison to a personal fitness training, either in a one-on-one or a class-training setup. Admittedly, the fact that clients are following instructions from the coach means it is slightly different to the executive coaching context, however the elements of accountability partnership, process discipline and process goals, planning and review, tracking and recording progress, and attitude role modelling are all analogous.

Most people I have asked about using a personal trainer have said there is no way they would have achieved even half of what they have without a specialist accountability partner who ensures that the agreed process is rigorously followed and that performance progress is tracked and visible. There is an investment in an optional service with results that are exponentially better than if the individual or team went without focused and specialist support: cost forgotten, benefit tangible and measurable.

Another great analogy for me is learning a new language. Assuming it is optional but potentially highly valuable (travelling and possibly working in another country), there is significant similarity there. Assuming there is a cost for the language coach, then that is similar. The coach or tutor will bring structure and a toolkit to accelerate learning and group work (if there is a class group), but ultimately the student or students will have to engage and commit (ownership, process, time) in order to realise course success. Once the language is learned, the coach can step away; the client is now independent and far more capable, more confident, and more effective for the long term. The return on initial investment is likely to be measurable and significant in terms of time and money saved through enhanced capability and efficiency: cost forgotten, benefit overwhelming.

Mostly, performance coaches help us do what we could do on our own but don't. What price should we put on a resource that helps us genuinely exceed our expectations and unleash our potential?

So, what is the elephant in the room? There needs to be a real appetite for excellence from the leadership team, and a willingness to consider investing in a deliberate initiative to catalyse team transformation.

Clear Process

I recently took time out to reflect on the key ingredients for excellence.

Leadership—Leadership or sponsorship is the beginning and the end of high performance. The style that I believe works best based on my observations is servant leadership as typified by Shackleton or Mandela: humble but resolute, set the example, walk the talk, influence through action, and inspire through vision.

Enrolment—Stakeholders need to be onboarded. People need to feel respected and heard. This is not a one-off event; it is an ongoing concern. Team members must feel that they are appreciated and are contributing links in the chain. Commitment stems from a sense of inclusion and collective inspiration.

Teamwork—Who better than the All Blacks rugby team to exemplify this ingredient? The team needs to be greater than the individuals involved; superstars like Richie McCaw and Dan Carter were not excused from sweeping the sheds. Being humble heroes is part of the legacy and the team integrity. High-performing teamwork involves the team members themselves holding each other to an ever-higher standard. The All Black saying goes, "Leave the jersey in a better state than when you were privileged enough to first pull it on."

Best Practice—This involves constantly benchmarking, analysing, and innovating leading indicators, work processes, tools, and behaviours for best results. British cycling is a pertinent example: Dave Brailsford championed the concept of marginal gains in every contributing aspect of overall performance so that tiny tweaks can lead to small wins, larger improvements, and ultimately a step change to a podium finish!

Recognition—Always recognise and reward standout effort, contribution, and achievement. A pat on the back with genuine sentiment from a respected leader to a valued team member is more significant than any prize money. The head coach of the Blitz Bokke once tweeted, "I would go to war for these guys." Heartfelt praise—high performance.

Reflection—Average teams don't bother to review past performance in any meaningful way; they tend to carry on doing things the way they've always been done. High-performing teams understand that in order to stay ahead of the competition, you must invest in continuous analysis, review, and introspection. It is the whole concept of lessons learned and learning implemented.

In combination, these six ingredients are a recipe for campaign success. A compromise on any of them will likely detract from high performance and allow the steady slide to mediocrity.

There are other ingredients and other ways of looking at the concept of high performance, but I hope this list provides some food for thought.

Current Reality

Conducting a formal client feedback process at the end of a performance-improvement intervention of any kind is essential.

End-user comments about where they feel and see the value helps to understand specifically what method is appreciated at the front line.

1. Disciplined approach to procedural adjustments that removes lost time and cost and enhances safety during the campaign.
2. Engaging all crew to participate in working improvements within a positive and constructive framework.
3. Capturing all lessons learned and giving feedback to the crews on their performance.
4. Identifying and capturing inefficiencies and then working team solutions before repeating the same activities again makes a big difference.
5. The way the risk register and lessons learned tracker are populated and then worked to closure, and the way these knowledge deposits are then forwarded to our next campaign, is the most valuable aspect of the methodology.

Project sponsors and end users appreciate the opportunity to provide honest feedback. End-user comments are very useful in helping to continually improve the accelerators to automatic excellence.

The value is clearly in the simple but essential

performance-improvement disciplines of rigorous planning, measuring, and learning, but more than that, the value is perceived in the crew engagement and the team enrolment. "One team, one mission" is key.

We aim to inspire ourselves and the crews with whom we work to unleash our collective potential. We do this with a bespoke method and a servant-leadership mindset. We never take clients for granted, and we seek to innovate in accordance to ongoing feedback.

Excellent performance coaching pays for itself many times over. Value, and not cost, is what should be remembered.

I have done many performance-climate assessments for the operational divisions of oil-and-gas companies. The assessment allows assessors to listen to those who are actually making things happen at the front line; we learn about the challenges they face, we ask about what could improve, we respect and collate the feedback to our structured questions, and we get a sense of the current reality for each project team.

In addition, we ask key stakeholders about their desired futures. We note the differences of opinion so that any misalignment can be addressed and debated through to an agreement on mission, vision, goals, and measures of success.

Without a performance climate assessment, there is insufficient reconnaissance to ensure that an approved coaching intervention is laser-focussed on the right areas to get the maximum return on effort.

A performance improvement campaign can transform

project performance from the current reality with all of its challenges and failings to a desired future which typically includes safe, profitable operations, achieving agreed objectives whilst maintaining team morale and rewarding individual commitment and contribution.

It all sounds simple and straightforward, but without a long-term transformation commitment from project leadership, the future reality will continue to be the current reality. Furthermore, transformation takes time; the return on the investment of money, energy, and effort will not be immediately apparent. Indeed, it will not materialise if the proven steps to genuine change, and specific priorities for each project team, are not addressed with uncompromising discipline.

The immediate priorities are also known as the low-hanging fruit. For us, these priorities are typically the most tangible improvements to enrol the front-line workforce to enable some early wins and to launch the transformation process. An example priority is either of the foundational layers of Maslow's hierarchy of human needs (welfare and/or safety). If there is a clear issue here, it needs to be resolved before further progress can be made.

I am passionate about unleashing the potential of a project team and helping the team to influence what they can in order to give high performance the best possible chance of success. It is why I do what I do.

In the commercial world, there is a very necessary focus on return on investment (ROI). An investor in a product or service must be convinced that the return justifies and ideally multiplies the investment—a proven "value add".

In today's world of instant gratification, it can sometimes be difficult to persuade investors that transformation can take time to achieve. I was inspired recently during an assessment when a key rig site supervisor talked about the absolute necessity to focus on team first: safety, ownership, initiative, and community spirit. While he was talking, I noticed a recently printed chart which showed that on a key divisional operational measurable, he had the best performing team. *No coincidence,* I thought. A genuine leadership investment in safety, teamwork, and process compliance had led to a best-in-class result after a year of hard work. In his words, "We didn't change any equipment; we changed our method and mindset." I learned that the team had gone from last to first.

With people and process, transformation takes time. It takes world-class leadership and team enrolment, commitment, consistency, and ongoing effort. However, we have seen time and again that determined leaders can enable the team to realise their collective vision, provided the right team is on the field and the right steps are followed with uncompromising discipline. The ROI is the desired future. It is as simple as that.

Accountability Partner

An accountability partner is a person who coaches another person in terms of helping the other person to keep a commitment. This can apply to teams as well as to individuals.

What is performance creep? This happens when standards start to slip over time. An example is a project where the team commits to a review after every operational phase. Perhaps after the third phase, the review does not happen due to a distraction. The next few phases are reviewed as planned, but then several are missed due to other distractions. By the eighth phase, no one is pushing for a review because it feels too much like hard work anyway. Sound familiar?

What about quality versus ticking the box? An example is committing to improve our fitness by going to the gym three times a week. In my experience, there is a big difference between attending a class or using a personal trainer versus training on my own. Class instructors or personal trainers will ensure that I am punctual, prepared, and completely focused. They also tend to provide motivation and objective feedback. Attending gym ticks the box; optimising my time there assures quality.

A performance coach is an accountability partner. Investing in the right project performance coach will guarantee the following.

- Minimisation or elimination of performance creep.
- Assured quality versus ticking the box.
- Motivation and objective feedback.

Accelerated improvement is a competitive advantage. An accountability partner will help drive the agreed inputs to achieve extraordinary results earlier than normal. Whether it is cost reduction through smart collaboration or body-fat reduction through smart training, investing in the right accountability partner has proven to yield an exponential return.

External Expertise

We are all a function of our upbringings and indeed the environments within which we have worked. Our structure of interpretation (SOI) is based on the reference points we have for how things should be done—or should I say, have been done in our previous experience. We know what we know, and that is familiar. Familiar is comfortable, so the temptation is to do things the way we have always done them.

It is startling how easily project teams' default to the way it has always been done. This default setting often includes the perspective that no external assistance is needed because "we can manage this in-house". Indeed, this perspective is often underpinned by budget constraints, spending cuts, or leadership insecurity.

The simple truth is that the right external resources will relieve your project team of burdensome administration whilst also objectively challenging the status quo.

What price can be placed on time freed up for key project personnel to focus on their core business expertise without distraction, and on critical path time saved thanks to consistently applied best-practice disciplines to get the best out of the assembled team?

In 2003, Clive Woodward coached England to Rugby World Cup glory in Australia. When interviewed in later years about what contributed to that achievement, Sir Clive often identified the importance of external expertise. His approach was to identify all the components needed to make an athlete or team excel, and then to engage the best external resource available to refine each of those components.

A proven expert in continuous improvement through accelerated team-building expertise and innovative learning know-how is surely an important consideration if high performance is the aspiration.

Performance Coaching

Evidence shows that the right focus prior to execution can ensure fewer mistakes are made early on thanks to risk mitigation, the application of transferable learning through shared experience, and rigorous challenge to the plan. On a drilling campaign, this means that the first well will likely be drilled more safely and more efficiently (cost effectively) than it would be if a less rigorous approach is taken during the pre-execution phase.

Applying this necessary rigour takes significant time and effort. In theory, it can be done by someone within the operator team. In reality, those individuals are already at capacity completing their own daily tasks and troubleshooting daily issues as execution mobilisation looms ever closer. A performance coach with relevant experience and bespoke tools, and who is accountable for harnessing the collective expertise of the project team and for ensuring risks and actions are closed in a timely manner, will significantly increase the chances of the project team getting the first well right the first time.

Evidencing the value of this rigorous approach can be done by calculating the time (and cost) saved through harnessed changes (captured and embedded lessons or suggestions) to the original plan, whether in the form of smarter technology, more efficient processes, or additional expertise. In most cases, upfront savings pre-execution more than pay for the coaching overhead for the entire project.

During project execution, leadership and team commitment and an uncompromising approach to the disciplines of advance planning and after-action review, as well as a regular lessons-learned conference call, undeniably accelerate the natural learning curve. This also enables a strong safety culture through communication, awareness, and teamwork.

Again, an ever-present, versatile coach who is embedded within the execution team and is accountable for capturing, tracking, and closing any and all opportunities on behalf of the team will drive a quantifiable improvement in efficiency (and cost reduction). This improvement would be slower without this resource, whose sole remit and focus is the implementation and utilisation of proven disciplines and tools, and which is not distracted by real-time operations management.

It is especially during the first several wells of a drilling campaign that the perfect storm occurs; the team is still settling into a new rhythm, problems are encountered for the first time, and lesson after lesson comes rolling in. It is at this stage that a qualified, driven, and experienced performance coaching resource delivers the multiple return on the initial investment. The reason for this is that the early lessons that are captured, tracked, and closed, and that apply to every subsequent well (often several times a well), will clearly save the most time (and cost) overall.

Not to belabour the point, but without an objective, dedicated resource who is focussed on this responsibility, it is very unlikely that the same level of rigour will be applied to capturing lessons, especially when troubleshooting occurs and everyone's attention is on finding a way to keep moving forward on the critical path.

As the project passes the midway point, we tend to see more consistent efficiency and diminishing returns on the improvement curve. Fewer learnings are captured after each repeated phase, and there is decreasing fluctuation in repeated performances.

Evidencing the value of the improvement process (and the investment in a performance-coaching resource) at the end of a project involves calculating the client-agreed savings from each advance planning meeting, closed and implemented lessons learned, and indeed each implemented suggestion that has typically been prompted by a support initiative and has enabled the team to work smarter (and safer).

The value proposition becomes increasingly clear, which is why contracts are often extended (to support a new scope or a new team).

When you consider that most projects have a combination of people (the wider project team), process (the way the team gets things done), and technology (the equipment necessary to do the work), it is reasonable to suggest that any project can benefit from a coach.

Engaging the right coaching service to support your project is a challenge in itself; the benefits of that engagement will also need to be clear and quantifiable.

There are two key benefits oft' repeated by investors in a performance solution.

- A credible and respected coach can help the team feel like a team before the going gets tough.
- Relevant coaching tools help the team effectively identify and implement measurable process improvements when the going gets tough.

These benefits have been acknowledged by clients dredging for offshore diamonds as well as clients drilling for offshore oil.

If you are part of a committed team with committed leadership, striving to go the extra mile and achieve the extraordinary against all odds, you can benefit from performance coaching.

Paradigm Shift

When we conducted our usual performance climate assessment to understand the challenges facing a client in readiness to execute an extremely important completions campaign, we discovered that their lessons-learned register for the two-year drilling campaign contained only one hundred lessons, and only 25 per cent of those valuable lessons had been closed.

Given the daily project spread cost of that operation, this meant that at least $3 million in project savings was sitting unrealised in an Excel file. Understanding this, we can further assume that only a portion of all the genuine lessons and opportunities for improvement had been captured in the first place. Conservatively, we can say that there could have been double the number of lessons in the tracker and, therefore, at least another $4 million in unnecessary repeated project costs.

That's $7 million minimum that could potentially have been saved through an under-$1-million investment in an enabled world-class performance coaching solution (coach plus tools) to guide robust lesson capture and closure (75 per cent plus closure on most projects after three months).

What about the bright ideas that our teams have for working smarter? If lessons are not being rigorously closed due to insufficient internal capacity, then it is a certainty that new ideas generated by team workers at the coal face will not be meticulously harvested, organised, and (where appropriate) implemented.

Our clients confirm that the reason for this is that their own teams are already at maximum capacity during the readiness-to-execute and execute phases, working fifteen-hour days and focussed on keeping operations moving forward safely.

In the current economic climate with a lower oil price and every effort to reduce operating costs, it would seem more important than ever to guarantee the capture and closure of lessons and to inspire the project team to submit regular ideas for additional savings.

This kind of initiative used to be considered optional but must surely now be considered essential: With the best will in the world, technical leaders cannot drive this on their own. They need support for two reasons: (1) the specific skill set required to successfully and continually engage the team on objective continuous improvement, and (2) the time required to administrate lesson and suggestion registers to the necessary standard for tangible benefit. Their focus must be on technical instructions and project leadership, already a full-time job.

Now is the time to promote efficiency and prevent unnecessary costs. It is time to ensure that the bright ideas from our teams no longer go unattended.

Sometimes in business and in life, we simply must consider the evidence, weigh the pros and cons, and then take a leap of faith.

Gut feel plays a role, and indeed, our attitudes will often dictate how our decisions play out.

It is like this with coaching. There will be evidence of the impact coaching has had elsewhere. There will also be positive and negative commentary based on different experiences and perspectives.

Ultimately, the investment decision will be a leap of faith, but with sound research, a considered choice of coach, and commitment to the process, our client feedback has repeatedly shown this to be a very rewarding investment well made.

Growth requires a paradigm shift. A step change in performance inevitably requires a new approach and, to some extent, a leap of faith.

Planning

There is much discussion about the value of a meeting (or meeting too often), but supposing a meeting is agreed as necessary, then to what degree do you extract every possible ounce of value from that meeting?

"Meeting 101" suggests nominating a chairperson and

a scribe, but all too often, neither role is conducted as well as it should be.

The engine of continuous improvement in the offshore oil-and-gas industry is powered by planning, reviewing, learning, and implementing lessons in time for the repeated task.

As such, the planning meetings, which focus on scrutinisation of the work instructions and agreement of offline preparation activities, are very important and saturated with critical information. The operational reviews are even more important given that their aim is to accurately capture and consider all lessons for subsequent closure.

Central to the value proposition of an expert performance coach in this environment is the disciplined facilitation of planning meetings and operational reviews. More often than not, the coach needs to set the scene for constructive meetings whilst also ensuring that maximum benefit is gained from the congregation of all key stakeholders.

In our experience, with the approval of the team, voice recording of the meetings is the only way to make absolutely sure that no vital nuggets of information go astray. Not only does this allow the performance coach to focus on the team dynamics around the room so that everyone has a voice, but also it means that when the recording is later transcribed, it can be repeatedly replayed to make absolutely sure that crucial detail is checked and understood.

Anything worth doing is worth doing well. The project team relies on a world-class performance coach to ensure that agreed meetings happen, to inspire the right culture at the meetings, and to enable a maximum return on the collective time invested in the get-together.

To add some context, on average, most end users agree that every planning meeting saves an hour of online operational time (>$25,000), and every review captures on average at least three quality lessons (more than three hours, or $75,000 saved). Typically, there are about two of each meeting per week, so there is a minimum of $200,000 in team savings every week if meetings are optimised.

Over and above the cost savings, team morale and project safety will benefit from professionally facilitated meetings, which produce valuable output.

In summary, optimising meeting value is potentially the most important aspect of your continuous improvement campaign.

Disruption

The word *disruption* seems to be increasing in popularity. Recently, it has been frequently used in the context of business and innovation.

It got me thinking about the concept and whether I could find a clear example of the impact of disruption. Let's start with a business definition: "to change the traditional way that something is done, especially in a new and effective way".

There is an excellent example from sport. In 1968, Dick Fosbury came up with the Fosbury Flop, clearing the bar backwards rather than forwards. It completely changed the way high jump was done, and it lifted performance over the next decade. The Fosbury Flop is now the standard.

Disruption apparently transcends innovation in that the latter tends to build on existing trends, whereas disruption can be unpredicted and unexpected whilst often causing a massive paradigm shift.

I then got to thinking about the performance coaching approach we have taken with clients and whether any of our embedded interventions have been truly disruptive. It was difficult to tell, but certainly one element of our toolkit, which aligns to the definition of "change in tradition plus new and effective", is the use of video and the building of a project video library for all operational sections, including key steps and lessons learned, in order to help project personnel to visualise safe, best practice, and teamwork.

We introduced this as one of our performance solutions on a deep-water drill ship in 2009, and though there was initial scepticism and surprise from some, there was also a measurable impact on safety and operational performance.

For this client, performance coaching was certainly a beneficial innovation with significant gains through proven best practice such as facilitated planning and review.

Arguably the disruption, which created a step change in front-line performance, came in the form of edited videos for all operations, including translated-text annotation for key lessons learned. Visualisation removed the language barrier, so crews collaborated with confidence and productive time increased by 20 per cent! This rig had never had an operational video library before.

A project video library for accelerated performance improvement is now a standard spoke in the Exceed transformation wheel, a disruptive Fosbury Flop!

Visualisation

Video has been around for a long time now, and with digital disruption in full force, it is certainly not a novelty. In this day and age, videos are super easy to create, edit, produce, and send. Yet the use of video to support performance improvement in heavy-industry operational environments is far from established.

My colleague Steve Blades introduced me to the concept of moviemaking as a fun, interactive, and genuinely beneficial event for corporate team building in South Africa sixteen years ago. I subsequently used it for group dynamics during executive breakaways and then introduced it to the deep-water offshore drilling world as a crucial spoke in our continuous-learning-and-improvement wheel back in 2008.

Explaining the value of video has become easier thanks to the various video channels on YouTube—for example, Food Tube, which is an online search-friendly instructional video recipe library which enables kitchen cavemen like me to learn how to cook an omelette. The point is that you can search for the recipe you need, and you can then watch the process evolve with verbal instructions, clear visuals, and best of all the ability to pause or rewind as needed.

The very same principle can be applied to upstream oil-and-gas operations. We have successfully built up rig-based video libraries on behalf of our clients so that all operations, inductions, drills, and celebrated achievements are captured to enhance learning, performance, consistency, and morale. Operational-section videos can be particularly valuable for inexperienced crews or front-line supervisors who have not done that activity for a long time.

Playing a comprehensive operational-phase video, with either soundtrack or voice-over, along with annotated commentary (translated as necessary) ahead of the same forthcoming operational phase subliminally prepares crew for what they will see and do. It mentally prepares operators for what to expect in the very same way that a safety video prepares passengers for a helicopter flight offshore.

We place such significance on this element of our continuous improvement toolkit because of the positive feedback we have received from our clients.

If a picture paints a thousand words, how many more words does a video equal? It is essential that videos receive oversight and expert quality assurance, as well as accurate annotation. This is where coaching expertise is required so that all parties are enrolled and involved in the initiative.

Provided this is professionally done, the value of video for continuous improvement is extraordinary: visually inducting crew into the safety culture saves lives; seeing what is happening helps the engineering team make million-dollar decisions; seeing how a job is done helps the drill crew save hours through learning, preparation, awareness, and efficiency; enabling workers to show their loved ones what they do and where they work boosts recognition and morale.

Safer, smarter, and more efficient operations performed by a more motivated workforce sounds like a reasonable value proposition. As part of a suite of tools designed to accelerate improvement on any project, it is a no-brainer.

Measurement

Invisible lost time (ILT) is the size of the opportunity to improve; it is the gap between current and potential performance. It is sometimes referenced as inefficient lost time. It is time during which progress is still being made on a task, but the progress is not as efficient as it should be. It is different from non-productive time, during which zero progress is made.

Interestingly, invisible lost time accounts for a significant amount of project time on most operations, yet it is often ignored or overlooked. On a two-well exploration drilling campaign, we focused on the first well's ILT, which represented 25 per cent of the total time taken!

A thorough analysis of this gap between planned and actual time revealed five significant areas for team focus on the second well. Because of that focus, the invisible lost time component was reduced from 25 per cent to 10 per cent, equivalent to approximately five million dollars of time and cost savings.

There can be several possible root causes for ILT. One is the possibility that the planned time was overly ambitious, in which case the ILT was not really ILT. But if this was the case, at least the variance and subsequent analysis would have alerted us to the fact that the planned time was unrealistic.

Other common root causes that I have come across over the last fifteen years include the following.

1. Inadequate pre-job communication and offline preparation.

2. Weak front-line leadership and poor delegation, which then allows poor teamwork.
3. Lack of crew experience and/or disparity in the experience of different crews.
4. Shortage of immediately available mechanical tools to optimise the job and troubleshoot critical path issues.
5. Indecision during execution.

We have discussed before that projects involve people, processes, and appropriate technology or equipment. Reflecting on the common contributors to inefficiency in oil and gas, we are reminded that though it is of course essential to have the right equipment on the rig floor serviced and ready to deploy, it is even more important that the right supervisors are in place with genuine leadership skills and a thorough understanding of the team and the plan, including contingency options in the event of trouble.

Inexperience requires mentorship and sometimes further training; if these elements are ignored, inexperience can quickly become incompetence and, in the worst case, lead to unnecessary incidents. This would be an example of invisible lost time (ILT) leading to non-productive time (NPT) due to a lack of attention and correction, when the warning signs first emerged.

In summary, invisible lost time is a silent budget killer, but worse than that, if left unchecked, it can kill morale and threaten personnel safety. Time after time, we have seen significant project improvement simply by ensuring that ILT is accurately measured, analysed, discussed, and addressed at root cause.

Performance coaches, if used, play a fundamental role in conjoining the office-based design team with front-line operators so that genuine ILT root causes can be established, and salient solutions can be embedded into revised programmes.

Learning

The correlation between leading and lagging indicators of performance is a fascinating one. Clearly, it is also hugely significant given that the lagging indicators are effectively the business results.

I reflected on this recently, albeit with a laser focus on the offshore oil-and-gas industry where I have advised on front-line performance improvement since 2008. Lagging indicators tend to be about safety, productivity, efficiency, and cost. Leading indicators tend to be about team induction and recognition, safety management participation, efficiency and cost-improvement contribution, planning, review, and closing the learning loop.

I trawled the data that we had collected in that time and realised it aligned with my intuition. On all projects, there had been clear evidence that improvement and innovation had benefited from a rigorous approach, but the difference between the good and great projects had been project leadership adherence to the regular weekly lessons-learned conference call.

On projects where there has been performance creep on this fundamental discipline, there has always been performance creep in other key areas as well. Operational reviews have typically slipped, and planning rigour has been eroded too. Ultimately, on projects where lip service was paid to the necessity for a weekly lessons-learned conference call between the office and the front line, trouble has continued to interfere with progress, and results have been inconsistent.

It is arguably the less tangible benefits of the weekly learning conference call that have the greatest impact, and these benefits are therefore most significantly missed when this discipline is dismissed. I am talking here about leadership cohesion, collaboration, camaraderie, mutual respect, and a sense of fun. These are soft elements that are hard to achieve and that emerge when stakeholders from different sides of the contract table go through the hard yards together and become one team with one mission.

An investment in a declared improvement initiative, as distinct from assuming that daily business as usual will naturally lead to improvement, is a declaration of intent. It is a signal to the project team that ordinary will not suffice. It is an investment in a project performance legacy. It is a project less ordinary and more extraordinary.

Weekly one-hour lessons-learned conference calls driven by the project leader convey the following key messages to the team.

1. We do the right thing.
2. We do what we agreed and committed to do.
3. Learning is important for everyone at every level of the operation because we don't know everything; in fact, we are all learning all the time.
4. Going into a repeat operation with a related lesson still open is unprofessional.

5. World-class results are driven by a world-class team which maintains the highest standard no matter what.

The engine of performance improvement includes planning, review, and closing the learning loop. The way these disciplines are applied may look different from one industry to the next, but they are fundamental to grow and learn. They require teamwork, communication, organisation, and attention to detail. They require effort.

Our project data conclusively shows that there is a very clear correlation between team adherence to rigorous, professional, weekly lessons-learned conference calls and the slope of the improvement curve for the key measurables of safety, time, and cost.

Capture, discuss, close, and implement lessons learned for next-time improvement, and you will raise the performance bar—guaranteed.

Let's discuss double-loop learning.

Double-loop learning is used when it is necessary to change the mental model on which a decision depends. Unlike single loops, this model includes a shift in understanding, from simple and static to broader and more dynamic, such as taking into account the changes in the surroundings and the need for expression-changes in mental models. (Wikipedia)

Wikipedia also makes available a diagram to illustrate the difference between single- and double-loop learning.

The difference is the change in the mental model based on feedback.

I really like this concept, and it completely applies to a recent adaptation I made to my nutritional approach.

My typical single-loop approach to eating for wellness used to be around reducing "bad carbohydrate" and sugar intake whilst increasing protein and good carbohydrate. The results were generally positive but not necessarily without perceived or real downside.

My double-loop epiphany related to new information and a revised mental model regarding the significance of "good fat" in my nutrition. Rather than applying the same rules to my decisions, I have revised my mental model and changed the decision-making rules regarding what I eat!

This kind of paradigm shift reminds me of the relevance of double-loop learning for champion teams. Rather than blaming problems outside their control, high-performing teams tend to adapt their mental models based on real-world feedback. They take massive action and influence key leading indicators within their control in order to succeed.

The following statement is often attributed to the famous scientist Charles Darwin: "It is not the strongest of the species that survives, nor the most intelligent. It is the one that is most adaptable to change."

If this is the case, double-loop learning is key.

Forgetting Curve

In his book *The Magic of Accelerated Learning*, Som Bathla reminds us of the "forgetting curve" which purports to show that humans tend to halve their memory of newly learned knowledge in a matter of days or weeks unless they consciously review the learned material.

Hermann Ebbinghaus created the forgetting curve in 1885. From this discovery, he came up with the effects of over-learning or relearning. It is not surprising to note that his experiments showed that the forgetting curve for repeatedly relearned material was shallower.

What we at Exceed Performance call the engine room of accelerated learning and performance improvement is based on the same premise. With client leadership, we implement the key discipline of frontline operational reviews as well as weekly lessons-learned conference calls between the front line and the management team. Captured and closed lessons are revisited during planning meetings for next time.

This then mitigates the known phenomenon of the forgetting curve in a high-risk, operational environment. Team reviews with follow-up minutes and reports promote efficiency and safety rather than leaving memory to chance.

The key to remembering what needs to be done is to implement a process to ensure that nothing is forgotten. Without reminder and regular review, research has shown that we retain little of what we first learned; less than 20 per cent after a month!

Don't forget to invest in a solution for yourself and your team.

Marginal Gains

Most of us are aware of the four-minute mile and the fact that no one in the world of track and field believed the four-minute barrier could be broken before Bannister achieved this feat in 1954.

The sub-four-minute mile represents a step change in the history of middle-distance running. The record stood at 4:01 for nine years, and yet once Bannister had broken the barrier, it was broken again within nine weeks!

It took many years for Bannister to create this step change in athletic perception. This was done through marginal gains as illustrated below.

Bannister's marginal gains to a step change in the 4-minute mile

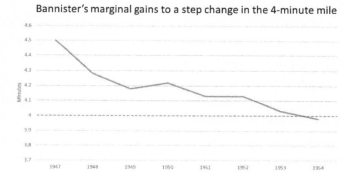

Not only did he demonstrate continuous improvement (with a few setbacks), but he also demonstrated what we now call marginal gains by targeting minutiae such as lighter running shoes and sharper spikes, as well as innovative training techniques such as fartlek and interval running.

Dave Brailsford, the cycling-performance director, recently popularised the concept of "marginal gains" and targeting 1 per cent improvements in everything that had even the slightest impact on a cyclist's performance in order to achieve the breakthroughs we have witnessed over the last five years in British cycling. He cited examples as random as better handwashing to prevent illness and consistent pillows for sleeping to emphasise the point that every tiny change for the better will potentially underpin a genuine step change in performance come the day of the race.

As a project performance coach, I find this most illuminating and a strong reminder that behavioural habits and process disciplines under our control are the strongest levers to achieve project success. We continually evolve our transformation methodology to cover all bases for incremental wins, no matter how small.

Marginal gains often seem irrelevant at the time, yet in hindsight, their contribution to the ultimate step change in perception and performance can be fundamental.

Capturing one lesson and making one safety observation a day on an oil rig can feel like a very marginal gain, yet we've seen this contribution scale up over a short time, and when every crew member is capturing a lesson and making an observation, a performance step change can be achieved. The micro gains take some sacrifice and extra effort; the step change in performance makes it all worthwhile.

Continuous Improvement

Continuous improvement sounds like a no-brainer, but the reality is that many of us like routine, and we struggle to make smart changes to how we operate.

It is for this very reason that the team needs to be heard. Essentially, this initiative invites all members of the project team to articulate work-specific challenges and suggest practical solutions. These suggestions are submitted to the performance coach, who records the submissions and then facilitates a regular session with key project leaders in order to focus attention on high-priority improvements that ultimately reduce time and cost, often on the critical path.

Typically, this initiative alone pays for the investment in an experienced and proven external resource to support continuous improvement. The initiative will gain traction only if project personnel feel recognised for their contributions and see their submissions being recorded and progressed. This administrative task requires discipline, diligence, and leadership support.

With the correct approach to enrolment and execution, teams can unleash their potential and make significant improvements in a short space of time. This is exactly what we saw on a two-well drilling campaign where the team saved over one million dollars by working smarter and safer, not harder. This saving came purely from front-line workers telling their leaders how their jobs could be done better and then having their leaders listen and actually do something about it.

Smart change requires the right appetite for change such that the right people step back and listen to the right ideas. This is easier said than done, but it is a no-brainer once in place.

Deliberate Practice

In 2017, CrossFit coach Ben Bergeron published a great book called *Chasing Excellence*, which focused on the 2016 CrossFit Games and particularly the two individual champions who were trained by Bergeron, Mat Fraser and Katrin Davidsdottir.

One of the concepts I found most intriguing in the book was deliberate practice. This approach involves stepping outside our comfort zones and trying activities beyond our current abilities. The approach can be broken down into four elements.

1. It is designed specifically to improve performance.
2. It is repeated a lot.
3. Feedback on results is continuously available.
4. It is highly demanding mentally and not necessarily enjoyable because it means we are focusing on improving areas in our performance that are not satisfactory.

Bergeron makes the point that the requirement for concentration is what sets deliberate practice apart from mindless routines and playful engagement. Hard work is not enough; it needs to be smart hard work!

All teams naturally improve over time, but you must get deliberate to make an early step change on a short campaign.

Single Tasking

I've always been a multitasker, and not necessarily a good one!

Recently, I've learned the value of single-minded focus on one task at a time as an approach to get more done.

I realised that one of the reasons my fitness has improved

is because when I go to the gym, I am not doing anything else. My single task for that hour is to get a workout done.

I've started to use that reference point to complete other tasks. For example, when back offshore for a hitch, I needed to get a video made. Rather than drag it out for hours while I did other work in parallel, I focused only on the video review and closed it out in a few hours before moving onto the next task.

I've realised that there is a very fine line between multitasking and selective distraction. Email at work is the classic example. TV is often the culprit at home.

In this age of instant gratification and information overload, single tasking has become a competitive advantage.

The ability to focus and to complete a demanding challenge takes discipline.

Discipline is easier when we are feeling determined. That tends to be after rest and refreshment, and as discussed elsewhere, as part of a routine.

Give it a go. Decide on the single task, remove distraction, determine your definition of *done* for that timeslot, and go get it done.

Simple! It is not always easy, but it is potentially very effective.

Appreciation

In the oil industry at present, there are many companies struggling as a result of COVID-19, a lower oil price, and an unpredictable recovery. The future is uncertain.

At times like these, team members naturally become

anxious about their own futures. Morale can suffer as staff search for reassurance and inspiration.

There are some crucial agreements which high-performing project teams have in place in order to drive excellence no matter what the weather outside. These principles should apply anywhere.

1. Meet regularly to maintain clear communication and team unity. Meetings need to be short, valuable, and well managed with a clear agenda, chairperson, and prompt, actionable output. Online gatherings have helped this discipline due to the need for punctuality, brevity, and attention.

2. Measure and display performance. Progress against agreed strategic objectives, and actual versus planned performance, matters to everyone in the team. Find a way to make it visible even if it is not always positive.

3. Draw on team innovation and creativity to continuously improve. Low morale tends to emanate from a sense of disconnect and disempowerment. A sense of contribution and value correlates with higher morale.

4. Recognise team members for a job well done. Look for reasons to praise team members; always keep the team accurately informed so that they can contribute and respond.

5. Communicate effectively. This is probably the toughest and most important principle to achieve. It involves listening with empathy as well as building

trust, yet genuinely effective communication is a competitive advantage in any team.

These principles are woven into a robust, continuous-improvement approach and are especially important during bad weather. It is essential to focus on unleashing the potential of project teams through process discipline and a positive mindset.

In my experience, nothing undermines and divides a team quite like blame. Blame generally involves declaring that someone or something else is responsible for a fault or wrong. Blame is also known as finger pointing.

The opposite of blame is praise, recognition, and commendation.

Think for a moment about the difference in community morale between a culture where the predominant approach is blame versus one where praise is practiced most often. Which culture is more appealing to you? If it's the former, perhaps it's time for some personal reflection.

Interestingly, one of the simplest catalysts for performance transformation at the project front line is that switch in emphasis from blame to recognition, from looking for what went wrong to looking for what went right.

The point is not that fault should be ignored; rather, it is that team members should take ownership for our own roles, our own contributions, our own weaknesses, and (when they happen) our own mistakes. In high-performance teams, this means that there is no need for blame because team members declare and own their mistakes before anyone else needs to say anything. Jocko Willink and Leif Babin talk about this in their book *Extreme Ownership*, an account of the US Navy Seals who overcame innumerable odds against insurgents in war-torn Iraq.

The Seals talk about managing up and down the chain of command so that miscommunication is avoided. Rather than blaming others, their approach is always to say, "What did I do to cause an issue?" and "What do I need to do to prevent a repeat?" If everyone takes this approach, mistakes go down, morale goes up, and success is achieved.

All too often in the modern boardroom, we notice leaders blaming poor results on anything but themselves. Especially disappointing is that we often see blame being apportioned to people who are not in the room.

It is not surprising that the most respected and inspiring leaders actively prevent blame and encourage ownership. Blame is a cancer that, if left unchecked, can decimate a team.

Perhaps we should all start with the question "What have I done to make a positive difference to the situation?" What a refreshing alternative that would be to the blame game.

Handling Pressure

As they say in the military, "No plan survives contact with the enemy."

When performance does not go according to plan, pressure can build. This is when procedures and coping mechanisms are essential.

Pressure equals force divided by area, so one way to manage project pressure is to troubleshoot issues as a team, thus sharing the problem, finding a solution, revising the plan, and moving forward once again.

We work with project teams to ensure that when problems occur, the team takes time to pause, step back, conduct root-cause analysis using a structured approach, and communicate effectively with all key stakeholders to get agreement before moving ahead.

Most of us can relate to the negative manifestation of pressure whereby project leaders can feel compelled to find a quick fix in order to move forward once again. The trouble with this is that the quick fix might briefly mask the root cause, which itself will likely recur if not correctly addressed.

One way to handle pressure when the plan fails is to anticipate and acknowledge it, and then step back, communicate as a team, and identify the true root cause. Facilitated root-cause analysis can help prevent quick fixes and can help build trust.

Reflection

As one campaign comes to an end and another makes an entrance, we often find ourselves reflecting on what happened, where we are now, and where we want to go.

My epiphany has been the degree to which I can learn and grow with a genuine and thorough reflection on the recent past.

Looking back at last project, I discovered several breakthroughs and could analyse what made the difference. It boiled down to smaller steps never compromised rather than big aspirations with insufficient progress markers to help build momentum.

There are always disappointments, of course, including work opportunities unrealised and an imbalance amongst competing personal priorities. Analysis of these has helped me to refine my approach to business development and connect personal goals so that, where possible, personal priorities can be achieved together.

Importantly, reflection can and should inspire self-respect, gratitude, and recognition. When things are not going our way, we tend to forget some of the positives. Time set aside for reflection ensures that recent achievements are noted and appreciated. It also highlights significant others who have provided love and support to us along the way.

The power of reflection is huge. It is an in-depth retrospect to help us get better. This principle is of course best practice for not just personal but also project improvement. Regular and rigorous performance reviews gather lessons from what went well and not so well. These learnings help teams get better at anything and everything that is sufficiently reviewed. The trouble is that there is no instant future performance warning for non-review, so we assume we are OK to dismiss the need for regular reflection when in fact, staying the same effectively means we are losing ground.

The value of structured reflection and performance review as a minimum is organised learning, accelerated improvement, appropriate recognition, and (in the case of projects) a more cohesive and effective team.

Method Accelerators

1. Identify your accountability partners. Consider a coach.
2. Ensure excellent facilitation of team workshops.
3. Start as you mean to go on.

4. Do the right thing.
5. Do what you agree and commit to do.
6. World-class people maintain the highest standards no matter what.
7. Successful people stick to proven habits and routines.
8. Familiar routines promote focus and composure.
9. Chosen productive time needs to be the best time for you.
10. Learning is important for everyone at every level of the operation.
11. Create the correct surroundings and conditions for high performance.
12. Marginal gains and incremental change will lead to step change.
13. Take a disciplined approach to procedural adjustments.
14. Identify and capture inefficiencies and then work on team solutions.
15. Invest in a visual platform to share knowledge.
16. Risks and lessons should be captured and worked to closure for the future.
17. Measure, illustrate, and display performance, even if the news is not positive.
18. Draw on team diversity, innovation, and creativity to continuously improve.
19. Recognise team members for a good job well done.
20. Treat effective communication as the competitive advantage it is!

DIAL 3

MOOD

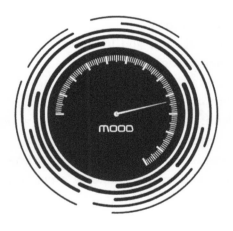

Mood is the background music, the ambiance, the feeling we have about an environment. Does it make us feel productive and energetic, or does it make us feel ignored and lethargic? In any team environment, one gets a sense of how people behave, how people are treated, and what is the state of morale. This all ties into the team mood, and this is fundamental to the acceleration of team performance from average to automatic.

I have been involved in dozens of team assessments in several sectors in the last twenty years, and there is one simple realisation which has been reinforced time and again through observation, perception, data analysis, and direct interviewee feedback.

The reinforced realisation is that even with old equipment and average process, a group of people with exceptional servant leadership and world-class teamwork will challenge, and often outstrip, similar operations which boast newer equipment and more advanced methodology.

Of course, if you take an exceptional team and give it the best processes and most advanced technology, in theory the sky is the limit. In reality, it is often the underdog label which inspires a benchmark team. Nonetheless, a well-led community of willing and proven volunteers with the right mindset and skill set is always preferable to a thousand pressed or egotistical men who lack motivation, drive, and cohesion.

There are indeed world-class organisations with the leadership, the team, leading technology, and a trail-breaking approach—great examples from which we should try to learn.

Sadly, all too often I have encountered the flip side: new installations with the latest hardware and software but a dysfunctional group of people. Without exception in these cases, there will be inconsistent and generally poor leadership. There will also be a collection of individuals, often very capable in their own right, who have not yet gelled as a cohesive unit and who are not yet striving to achieve a clear mission together.

My view is that it can be extremely difficult to help

build a high-performing operation; there is no doubting that. But the first step, as with any transformational journey, is admission that people are the most important component of any performance. Unless an investment is made in building a committed and well-led team, high performance will remain an elusive goal.

The founders of Performance Climate System (PCS) – an organisation which measures culture, engagement, and the impact of leaders on team performance – summarise mood as follows: "Leaders, motivated by their own personal drivers and influenced by the organisation they work in, create the climate in a team. The better the climate the greater the performance of that team."

Evoking Excellence

At some point or another, we should all confront some questions: "What am I passionate about?" "What makes my heart sing?" "What work was I born to do?" We reflect on our achievements, our strengths, and ultimately what we are passionate about. Posed another way, we ask, "What inspires me? What stirs my soul?"

A high-performing team is one where all the team members feel that they are drawing on their strengths most of the time each day. It is one where team members feel that they have voices and that their opinions really count. It is also one where team members feel fully enrolled and informed. Stakeholders in the right environment will feel energised to contribute because what they are doing has intrinsic and extrinsic benefit. The narrative is about value, not cost. In addition, there is a bond of trust and commitment—true collaboration.

Project leaders should create the conditions for this reality. Ideally, each specialist should be able to focus on his or her piece of the puzzle whilst appreciating the bigger picture thanks to clear communication. Supervisors should be inspired to unleash team potential. The continuous improvement process should become business as usual because it intuitively feels right. Process excellence should be streamlined and driven by someone who clearly loves this aspect of the role. This frees up the enrolled and informed technical experts to focus on their tools and their turn on the critical path. Inevitably, this leads to better project results.

Joining a new and diverse team, earning my place through congruent service and inspiring facilitation, and then being privileged to join the arduous climb to peak performance whilst supporting the journey and telling the story along the way—that stirs my soul. When you see the view from the top of the mountain, you forget the pain of the climb!

Safety

The right team mood can mitigate identified behavioural traps, as described here.

> Fear of perceived leadership pressure and peer pressure. A way to allay this fear is by constantly acknowledging the issue and consistently promoting an empowered climate whereby everyone feels comfortable to stop the job if something feels or

looks dangerous. This acknowledgement and promotion should be done at well-facilitated operational planning and review meetings where safety and operational leaders, and any other team members, are able to effectively communicate expectations.

Lack of awareness. A way to build awareness is by working tirelessly to ensure key information is visible, accessible, understandable, and transferable. Verbal communication is essential, but this can be complemented by poster campaigns, video messages, and other digital media.

Loss of concentration. A way to maintain concentration is by inspiring a high-performance team with a strong work ethic and a strong sense of loyalty and accountability between all team members. Toolbox talks immediately before a task should focus everyone, but ultimately the culture will drive consistently high levels of concentration.

Inaccurate risk assessment. There are no shortcuts to the comprehensive interrogation of project risk; a user-friendly but robust risk register is necessary pre-execution to ensure that all risks identified at the key risk awareness sessions are captured, extensively discussed by experienced subject-matter experts, and controlled to the greatest degree possible. This detail can then be filtered according to forthcoming tasks and included in planning meetings so that risks are clearly understood and addressed on the rig floor prior to execution.

Coaching and discipline can tackle human factors and enable safer operations. Performance leaders, who are sought out for their positive impact, should drive the agreed performance-improvement disciplines and engage with the workforce to help keep the team as safe as possible. High-performing teams are safe teams who are also emotionally intelligent.

To create a team mood that enables world-class performance, the following behaviours should be evident from frontline leaders.

1. Be positive and avoid negative talk.
2. Look for what went right and recognise contributors to that result.
3. Demonstrate an exemplary work ethic.
4. Keep your word and do what you say you will.
5. Be situationally aware always.
6. Be interested in what others have to say.
7. Embrace diversity and give everyone a voice.
8. Encourage team accountability to stick to our agreements.
9. Be authentic.
10. Be humble.

This is clearly not an exhaustive list, and nor is it always achieved by all team members at all times on all projects. However, this list provides a foundation for respectful servant-leadership on any continuous improvement campaign. In addition, it will unleash the latent potential of a high-performance team.

> "A leader is best when people barely know
> he exists, when his work is done, his aim
> fulfilled, they will say: we did it ourselves."
> —Lao Tzu

Behaviour

People often ask me about the best initial indicators of a team performance culture based on first impression: I always answer that it is about the simple basics; good or bad, these indicators are typically representative of the overall performance picture.

The first indicator is whether or not members of the organisation are audibly bad-mouthing management or each other. It is amazing how prevalent this is, and therefore the absence of negative talk is notable.

The second indicator is whether meetings happen as advertised and on time. Unfortunately, many organisations struggle to start meetings on time and to keep meetings effective. Consistently punctual and valuable meetings are therefore significant.

The third indicator is whether people do what they say they'll do when they say they'll do it. All too often, incongruence is the norm: someone promises to get something done but then needs constant reminding. Early delivery on small promises is a massive positive.

Performance culture has much more complexity, but these initial indicators have served me well for many years.

Here are some of the subtle behavioural indicators of a true team in any setting, of a team much more likely to achieve a high-performance culture, based on my observations and experience.

The first element is basic courtesy. This is such a fundamental one. It manifests in various daily interfaces, such as greeting colleagues when you see them and responding to communications in a timely fashion. It needs to be a two-way street; if it feels like one party is constantly having to initiate the courtesy, there is no true team.

The second element is basic trust. This builds on courtesy. A true team has formed and stormed to the extent that trust has been earned. It allows for personal growth and for individual expression to benefit the collective. If concerns about trust are regularly voiced, or micromanagement is in evidence, there is no true team.

The third element is basic empathy. This builds on courtesy and trust. It means that team members are interested in the challenges of colleagues and that they seek to understand different points of view. If there is no sense that team mates genuinely care or can step into the shoes of others, there is no true team.

The fourth element is basic energy. This is an essential ingredient in any successful team. Energy can be seen and sensed, as can lethargy—an opposite element synonymous with poor performance and disjointed teams. If there is a lack of energy, there is no true team, or at least not one that is likely to achieve high performance!

Bringing it all together; in my experience, true teams consist of courteous individuals with high levels of trust, genuine empathy, and high energy. These elements can be detected in a relatively short space of time. Deficiencies in any of these areas will detract from team togetherness and prevent high performance. Get the basic elements in place and build a true team.

I am a big fan of the quote "Everybody is a genius. But if you judge a fish by its ability to climb a tree, it will live its whole life believing that it is stupid".

We all have strengths and weaknesses. The founder of CrossFit, Greg Glassman, is quoted as saying, "Hiding from your weaknesses is a recipe for incapacity and error." I think this is also an important point, especially in the context of physical fitness.

My view is that a project team will deliver best results if the individuals within the team are in positions which draw on their demonstrated and appreciated strengths, and if those same individuals are continually striving to improve themselves, including awareness of, and attention to, personal weaknesses.

When I completed my full-time MBA at the Graduate School of Business (GSB) in Cape Town in 2001, I was part of a syndicate of about eight students throughout the year; halfway through the year, the syndicates were reshuffled in order to change the dynamics and force new collaboration. In the first instance, we were a dysfunctional team and failed to divide tasks according to individual strengths. In the second syndicate group, we were much more effective at ensuring that we allocated and accepted work in accordance with our interests and experience. My first syndicate consistently propped up the bottom of the academic tables, and my second was consistently towards the top. There was an element of general learning and improvement throughout the student body, but there was also a specific focus in our second group on leveraging the individual strengths available. The impact was measurable and unquestionable.

I was subsequently involved in designing and overseeing an annual breakaway for the new MBA syndicates of the full- and-part-time GSB programmes. Our aim was to compress and accelerate the natural team-building curve by putting the groups under different types of pressure in a fun outdoor environment and providing multiple reference points for dynamic awareness and integration so that syndicates commenced the academic curriculum as an established team, aware of individual strengths, and beyond the issues that often delay constructive bonding. The GSB has seen a noticeable drop in syndicate dysfunction as a result of this continued annual initiative. Students have responded that they feel the upfront breakaway eradicates ego and posturing and reveals individual strengths and weaknesses within hours. This is then a springboard to team effectiveness, enjoyment, and the smart division of tasks.

Understanding and promoting individual strengths within a project team tends to lead to harmony and high performance. There are many tools available to identify individual strengths, and the right one for your team is probably a smart investment.

Morale

There are three key reasons why morale matters on a performance-improvement campaign.

1. Safety is paramount, and low morale is generally linked to variable concentration and interest levels,

which means that the likelihood of a safety incident significantly increases as morale decreases.

2. Energy and productivity are linked to a positive attitude, which itself relies on good morale. By contrast, apathy tends to go hand in hand with depleted morale, so better morale aligns with better output.

3. Collaboration relies on good team spirit. Team spirit is affected by team morale. Collaboration is essential for effective planning, execution, review, and learning, so without good morale, each of these elements will suffer.

This is a deliberate simplification of a bigger subject, but I hope it conveys the obvious: ignorance of project-team morale is a risk, and ignorance of poor morale is negligent because good morale is essential for safe, productive, and collaborative operations.

A "one team, one mission" ethos has a noticeable impact on team morale and is a top-three contributor to project success.

Clearly morale does matter, and we've been privileged to support client leaders in bringing it about on challenging projects involving new teams, new regions, and new rigs. It is a critical success factor on any project and should always be top of mind.

Language

Much has been written about the language we use. When I completed my professional coaching course, one of my prescribed books was *You Are What You Say* by Larry Rothstein and Matthew Budd. In this excellent book, Dr Budd explains that our words play a major role in determining, not just reflecting, our health and well-being. He explores how the body learns many of its reactions, consciously and unconsciously, through language.

In my view, the language that we use as leaders also influences the team dynamic and human behaviour; workers and followers conform to the subtle cues of their management. Our words play a major role in team health and team well-being.

Two words that can have a disproportionately negative impact on morale and performance are *I* and *they*. Thankfully, a word that can undo that damage, if adopted as a better replacement, is *we*.

All too often, I have experienced the disappointment of hearing "I will decide" when it should be a team decision, or "they messed up" when in fact we were all involved somehow.

Incredibly, very little is lost, but a huge amount is gained if instead the message is, "We messed up, and we will decide how to improve together."

I have been on so many projects where the ubiquitous "they" are to blame that I wonder whether "they" have ever done anything right!

How about a switch to a world where the only time we use *I* or *they* is to say, "I made a mistake," or, "They did an excellent job." Otherwise, use *we* to include team and togetherness.

Based on the *we* cultures I've been privileged to serve,

you'll be amazed at the positive impact on morale and performance that this subtle shift can have.

Building a team takes time, energy, and expertise. It requires leadership and teamwork. It also requires a shared vision, mission, and shared values. Investing in getting it right yields a clear return.

On a campaign that Exceed led in West Africa 2018, there was a strong focus on all of the requirements listed above. At the planning workshop, some powerful questions were asked, and campaign supervisors shared their vision and values before challenging the draft programme in order to make it as robust as possible.

Below is the word-wall representing the project team's aspirations, focus, and values.

It was no accident that this collaborative early focus led to a world-class performance: the well was drilled safely and compliantly, ahead of time, and significantly under budget, with all objectives achieved.

Einstein was once asked how he would spend his time if he was given a problem upon which his life depended, and he had only one hour to solve it. He responded by saying he would spend thirty minutes analysing the problem, twenty minutes planning the solution, and ten minutes executing a positive outcome.

This relative emphasis on preparation and planning (prior to the execution phase) is as important for building a strong team as it is for building a robust programme for operations. The two need to be done in parallel.

Certainly, team feedback at the end of this successful campaign was that the outstanding results were a reflection on the leadership, the rigorous and collaborative planning, and the professional team-building emphasis in advance of operations. Team members from all parties felt heard, respected, and involved. This created a mood of confidence going into the campaign.

Performance Culture

The book *Coaching for Performance* is a great place to start when reviewing the literature on performance coaching and its background. Sir John Whitmore authored the book, which is now in its fifth edition (2017). It was first released in 1992 and was one of the first books on coaching in the workplace.

Whitmore learned about the *Inner Game* from Timothy Gallway, who pioneered the emphasis on "mind over matter" for sports competitors (with a focus on tennis, skiing, and golf), and subsequently for the workplace as well.

Whitmore went on to form Performance Consultants, and together with his associates, he co-developed the GROW model, which is one of the best known in the coaching world.

GROW stands for goals, reality, options, and will. It serves as an appropriate and easy acronym for coaches and leaders to use when coaching anyone.

In this book, Whitmore describes coaching as "creating the conditions for learning and growth". He talks about "unlocking our potential to maximise our performance" and draws on the acorn analogy whereby any acorn has the potential to become an oak tree if nurtured and nourished in the right environment.

He also references a superb formula, $P = p - i$ (Performance equals potential minus interference). I love the word *interference* in this context because it perfectly describes many of the real and imagined obstacles that we allow to detract from our own true potential.

> "Coaching focuses on future possibilities, not past mistakes." —*Coaching for Performance*

For aspirant coaches and leaders, this book is a must-read. It ultimately inspires a high-performance culture, and as Peter Drucker said, "Culture eats strategy for breakfast!"

As a performance coach myself, I was inspired by the book, and I particularly enjoyed the way Whitmore weaved in commentary about associated models relating to leadership, teambuilding, continuous improvement, goal setting, and the search for meaning and purpose.

> "If there was only the "right" way to do something, Fosbury would never have flopped!" —*Coaching for Performance*

Unlock potential, remove interference, transform, and transcend!

I recently came across the performance curve as developed and described by Performance Consultants International with Sir John Whitmore. The focus is on building a high-performance culture, and the stages progress from impulsive to dependent and independent, to interdependent. Low performance is associated with dependence due to the interference of elements such as dictatorship, over-regulation, apathy, blame, and a lack of empowerment and ownership. High performance is associated with independence to interdependence, as potential is unlocked, and true synergy is unleashed.

This model has parallels with Covey's observations regarding the progress leaders and teams make from dependence to interdependence, as well as Maslow's hierarchy of needs whereby self-actualisation releases our individual and collective creative potential.

Interestingly, when we consider the stages involved in the development of a learning culture, there is a clear similarity, which is the halfway line—the point on the journey when we sufficiently reduce interference to allow potential to flourish, and the point at which we achieve confidence through conscious competence in what we do and how we do it.

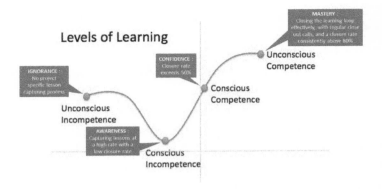

A final model to consider when studying team development to high performance is Tuckman's model, which I have accelerated below with the incorporation of a deliberate learning initiative: team leaders discuss key learnings and ideas on a regular basis to reduce the time taken to achieve full potential.

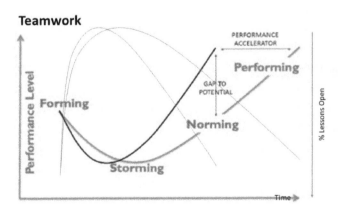

By overlaying these improvement models, one on top of the other, we arrive at some valuable conclusions.

1. There is a tipping point in team performance improvement that requires individuals to own a performance mindset, conscious competence, and a deliberate focus on assimilated learning.
2. There is a challenging transition that needs to take place. Once guidelines are agreed and implemented, empowerment and individual potential need to be nurtured. This includes necessary interference, awareness that the team has gaps, and constructive engagement (including some fierce conversations) to achieve high-performance interdependence.
3. There is a risk that once the transition past the tipping point has taken place, leaders and teams get comfortable and confident with above-average performance, rather than constantly stretching beyond comfortable to true interdependent mastery. In addition, it requires constant focus to maintain mastery.
4. This is where the power of habit is essential. In order to master performance at a higher level, the necessary habits need to be ingrained; otherwise, they will fall away. Robert Glazer of Acceleration-Partners recently posted about this: To help habits to become ingrained, the micro and macro environment should be set up to reduce interference with those habits. An example of this for me is having my latest audiobook ready to play, such that as it connects to my car audio when I start the car

to drive somewhere, I am immediately listening to insights which help me grow as a leader and coach. Create, maintain, and evolve the conditions to unlock full potential such that it is less about willpower and more about autopilot.

Project team performance facilitation involves an expert resource and a proven system to help leaders drive the transformation illustrated above. From impulsive to interdependent, and then the habits to sustain excellence; less interference, and more unlocked potential. A system driven by an objective expert resource is the uncompromising "automatic" process discipline for a high-reliability project team. This ingrains the necessary focus to maintain mastery.

In many parts of the world, oil goes hand in hand with instability and conflict. Fighting to secure control of significant oil reserves is a familiar story. Indeed, the oilfield has effectively been a battlefield in many regions for many decades.

There are other parallels too. A small percentage of oilfield workers have done some time on a battlefield somewhere. The work environment appeals: geographic frontiers, as well as high-cost, high-risk operations requiring resourcefulness, leadership, teamwork, and perseverance to succeed.

In recent times, there have been many oil companies battling to survive. COVID-19 and the oversupply of oil along with a disconnected strategic and political agenda has negatively affected the oil price and resulted in delayed and cancelled projects. This in turn has impacted the value chain and caused many companies and thousands of professionals to cease working in the oilfield.

As a former marine and current performance coach, I recognise and respect the significant efforts made by oilfield professionals daily and globally. Rig teams often battle weather conditions, logistical challenges, technical problems, crew diversity, and local hostility in order to make things happen and to get the job done.

Five transferable leading-success factors applicable to the battlefield and to the oilfield are as follows.

1. One team, one mission.
2. Respected leadership.
3. Thirst for learning.
4. Applied best practice.
5. Unwavering commitment.

With these factors as a genuine aspiration, the chance of successfully achieving goals and objectives is exponentially increased. Battling to victory against enemy forces, market forces, or the forces of nature takes considerable and coordinated effort. Tough times call for tough people and tough decisions, but they also call for tailored solutions to troubleshoot specific obstacles.

With some battlefield and some oilfield experience, like many others, I see some similarity and an opportunity to benefit performance through shared reality. The conversation continues.

Progressing from low performance to high performance requires honest and frank conversations which confront reality and acknowledge failure. The mindset and toolkit to enable this culture ensures that continuous improvement can thrive, and true learning can take place. It sounds straightforward but never is.

One of the phenomena that can derail an improvement campaign is something called cognitive dissonance. In simple terms, this is the discomfort experienced by an individual who holds two or more contradictory beliefs, ideas, or values at the same time; performs an action that is contradictory to their beliefs, ideas, or values; or is confronted by new information that conflicts with existing beliefs, ideas, or values.

If we zoom in on the final point and consider it in the context of a learning campaign where this notional individual is a key leader, it can be a real blocker to progress, but even worse, it can be dangerous.

In his book *Black Box Thinking* by Matthew Syed, he provides some seriously concerning examples of cognitive dissonance. One involves a senior surgeon who refuses to change his latex gloves for other gloves despite a junior anaesthetist advising him that the patient is experiencing a latex allergy (and could die). The other reminds us of the issue of weapons of mass destruction (WMD) in Iraq and the fact that Western politicians for a long time refused to accept that there were none. In both cases, the embedded, existing beliefs of key leaders made it almost impossible for them to accept new evidence because they conflicted too starkly with everything these people believed or had experienced, heard, or seen before.

I have facilitated some challenging conversations during which key project leaders have struggled to accept lessons learned, new ideas, practices, or even data because they have always done or perceived things a certain way. It reminds me of the old phrase "Because we've always done it like that".

We tend to look for evidence which supports our own beliefs. It is sometimes hard to accept that what we have believed for so long is, in fact, inefficient or even obsolete. We are seeing this play out in 2020 as governments attempt to find the right response to the unprecedented nature of the COVID-19 outbreak.

I used to believe that fitness training on my own was most cost-effective and efficient because I wasn't paying anyone, and I knew what I wanted to improve. The concept of a personal trainer or class instructor used to be dissonant for me, because I felt I had the qualification and motivation to train on my own, yet I was reading and hearing more and more about the benefits of external expert support. Eventually I altered my perception, and for the last ten years, I have acted accordingly and seen significant personal fitness benefit through personal training and now CrossFit class workouts.

Cognitive dissonance can be a block to improvement, and we should be aware of that!

Liverpool

I grew up in Southern Africa supporting Liverpool because Zimbabwean Bruce Grobbelaar was the flamboyant goalkeeper during the 1980s heydays of Liverpool football.

Recently I watched *Kenny*, which documents the footballing career of Liverpool legend Kenny Dalglish, including the Hillsborough disaster in 1989. This film is incredibly moving and inspiring at the same time. It sheds light on the heart of the Liverpool supporters' community while also highlighting some of the heroes of LFC in the last fifty years.

Steven Gerrard is arguably the most famous Liverpool player of recent times, and his involvement in the 2005 Champions League victory, "The Miracle of Istanbul", will live long in the memory. Gerrard has given many interviews about what Liverpool means to him. In his movie *Make Us Dream*, he talks about captaincy, responsibility, loyalty, and legacy.

Recently, Liverpool have had another resurgence, this time built around their inspiring coach, Jurgen Klopp.

Klopp is a special kind of coach. From my observations, he walks the talk on three critical themes.

1. He is the man "in the arena", Klopp is on the field whenever he gets a chance. You sense when watching Liverpool play that whatever the weather, and for better or for worse, Klopp is all in. He is part of the team, not separate from the team.

2. He tells the truth, but the glass is always half full. Klopp has earned respect from fans, competitors, players, and the media alike because he maintains a fair balance between honesty and optimism. For example, when it was mathematically impossible for Liverpool to win the Premier League, Klopp focused all his positive energy on winning the Champions League, which he always believed Liverpool could do, in 2019.

3. He always maintains his dignity and humility. Klopp embodies the saying "Humble in victory and

gracious in defeat". He is therefore a benchmark coach who strikes a near perfect balance between fierce determination and friendly demeanour, hunger and humour, excellence and empathy.

Klopp creates the best conditions possible for those around him to unlock their potential.

Clearly the 2019 Liverpool team had exceptional players, but games like the Champions League Anfield semifinal, when Liverpool beat Barcelona 4-0 to go through and win the final, showed that there is an X factor as well. Most 2019 LFC fans will tell you that the X factor can now always be seen cheering, encouraging, energising, and believing from the dugout.

Liverpool's lead on the premier league 2020 is testament to their "3M" excellence. They have mastered the best elements of mindset, method and mood, while demonstrating world-class leadership, teamwork, and discipline. Klopp has been central to creating the right mood at the club.

Blitzboks

The South Africa 7s team once again sits towards the top of the IRB 7s world series standings. They are always combative and continue to play a brand of rugby which thrills fans and neutrals alike.

The word *blitz* means an intense and sudden attack, an onslaught or bombardment, and it perfectly describes the way the Blitz Boks play each game. Physically they have smaller players than squads like Fiji, but in every other way, they are larger than life. There is an extraordinary energy and ferocity to their approach, extreme commitment to the cause, and passion and panache to boot.

If we consider the lagging indicators of high performance within the Blitz Boks setup, we easily note the following: consistently top three in the world and winners of the IRB 7s Series 2017 and 2018, phenomenal skill level, world-class commitment, behaviour of a close-knit family, visible elation when competing and performing at the highest level.

If we then consider the leading indicators to understand the culture which is contributing to these consistently exceptional results, we can draw from a 2016 blog post by Werner Kok (voted World 7s player of the year 2015).

> It really was a dream come true. Being part of this team means you have a small family who always has your back. They always support you and always push you to reach your goals. Believe me when I say, I have one of the best jobs in the world!
>
> Working hard and giving it our all at practice really paid off on game day. It's a case of input equals output. We were strong and consistent until the end. The best moment of this tournament was making the dream team with my captain, Kyle Brown. If you ask any one of the players, they would tell you how much it meant to me. It's the best feeling to see my name with some of the best players in the world. I'm going to continue to train hard, play hard, and help my team to victory, and try and make that dream team again.

Their style of play stems from a self-belief and camaraderie which is clear. Most important, the Blitz Boks inspire spectators around the world because they are achieving high performance whilst clearly enjoying themselves; they are as prepared as they need to be to perform on the world stage.

The bedrock of a world-class team performance blitz is a dream-team champion mood.

CrossFit

CrossFit does not appeal to everyone, but in fairness, most forms of physical endeavour provide similar lessons to business and life.

My experience with CrossFit is that there are some key elements of the general climate which have transferable value for continuous-improvement campaigns in any setting.

1. The most significant element is the sense of community which is built upon a shared passion and commitment to get better through determination and perseverance. More than that, there is a real focus on listening and learning from each other based on different techniques and personal triumphs over adversity.

2. Most CrossFit boxes have their rules somewhere visible; these include two very relevant points for aspirant champions: (a) leave your ego at the door, and (b) always be on time. At the top level in this sport, there is a genuine humility and discipline which inspires the average enthusiast to strive for improvement.

3. What gets measured gets managed. There is a genuine attention to data and detail in CrossFit; numerous apps have emerged over the last year which enable easy mobile capture and analysis of each workout so that comparison can be made with peers and personal history. Data analysis drives planning and programming while workout reviews contribute more data; this in turn drives quantifiable continuous improvement.

4. Encouragement and recognition, where needed and where it is due, become second nature because they are the right thing to do. Fitter, faster athletes make a point of cheering on less experienced enthusiasts as a matter of course. This engenders a sense of confidence, trust, and mutual respect throughout the community.

5. Everyone clears up after themselves no matter who they are. There is a real sense that every member of the community contributes to the quality of the experience and the workout environment. This attitude and action is led by the coaches. It underscores the fact that no matter how fit the athlete, the box is bigger than any individual.

There are clearly some very transferable lessons from CrossFit to continuous improvement campaigns in general: create a community, drop the ego, be punctual, measure performance, encourage and recognise others, and serve the community to make it better.

Spartan Way

I recently finished *The Spartan Way* by Joe De Sena. What a breath of fresh air. I recommend it to anyone who is interested in a warrior mindset, interested in raising standards, and keen to be inspired by a courageous tribe of humans.

De Sena is the energy behind the Spartan Race concept: Endurance and obstacle course races which test the human spirit and push human limits. He is worth listening to because he has successfully achieved extraordinary results by living the Spartan way.

He unpacks the ten principles of the Spartan ethos in ten separate chapters. I will summarise each based on what impacted me most.

1. Find our true north—self-awareness. True north strikes me as a superb euphemism for personal purpose. Once the mission or purpose is crystal clear, it is a simple case of testing any task against the obvious criterion: "Is this bringing the team/ me closer to or further from our/my true north?" Ironically, in the real world of navigation, there is magnetic north and grid north. Both are necessary for reasons we will not explore right now, but the fact remains that as with purpose-navigation, there is only one true north to the North Pole.

2. Make a commitment—perseverance. Worthy journeys are never easy. Whether it is marriage, mastery, or migration, it takes patience, sacrifice, and concerted effort over a long period of time.

Staying the course leads to a greater return on investment.

3. Fuel our enthusiasm—passion. Create the right conditions to unlock potential. Develop our strengths but address our weaknesses too. Embrace the process. It is simple but not necessarily easy.

4. Delayed gratification—discipline. Focus on what we want most, not what we want now. Resist the cravings and ignore the distractions; stick to the mission and vision.

5. Maximise our time—prioritisation. Time is precious, so use it wisely. Prioritise activities and endeavours which make a direct contribution towards fuelling our purpose. Be on purpose.

6. Get gritty—grit. Be resilient. Resilience is the number one predictor of success. It trumps talent every time. Don't quit anything worthwhile, ever.

7. Embrace adversity—courage. Every challenge is a marginal gain in confidence and credibility. Each obstacle is a potential reference point for self-respect and societal contribution.

8. Adjust our frame of reference—optimism. Everything in life is a matter of perspective. We get to choose how we frame an experience. We can't influence everything, but we can influence how we respond to what life throws at us. Be positive. Be kind. Be open to learning.

9. Be honourable—integrity. Do the right thing even when no one is watching—and especially when no one is watching. When we do the right things, the right things happen.

10. Be Spartan—wholeness. Become our best selves, individually and collectively. Be grateful, be helpful, be prepared, be awesome, and be Spartan!

There is a memorable section in this book when the author describes a proposal from two potential partners in a business venture. De Sena explained to these guys that he had a morning routine congruent with his true north, and if they wanted to convince him of their proposal, they should join in. His routine involved hours of burpees and other physical exercises which would have dissuaded most. But these men accepted the offer, travelled a long distance, participated in the ritual, and earned De Sena's respect through their attitude and effort.

De Sena recognised the Spartan spirit in these prospective partners. He observed the ten principles in action. Their mindsets were clearly aligned, and they have since joined forces on a successful venture. They had collaborative DNA, which is key for a true team.

True north equals vision and mission. These Spartan values equal solid milestones along the way.

Spartan teamwork was immortalised in the movie *300*, when they faced the Persian Army in the battle of Thermopylae. Although the story may have been embellished for dramatic effect, the Spartan people were undoubtedly feared and admired for their discipline and tradition. Their mood was always confident, even in the face of overwhelming odds at Thermopylae.

A confident mood is one based on a winning mindset, and a proven method. The Spartan way still stands as a prime example of exactly that.

Mood Accelerators

1. Drucker: "Culture eats strategy for breakfast!"
2. The most significant element is the sense of community.
3. Create the conditions for excellence. One team, one mission.
4. Build a sense of belonging.
5. Encourage collective contribution to vision and values.
6. Clear and visible charter of organisational purpose—your why.
7. Shared ownership of outcomes.
8. CrossFit: "Leave your ego at the door."
9. Be positive and avoid negative talk.
10. Listen to hear and understand.
11. Promote situational awareness from everyone.
12. Give everyone a voice.
13. Encourage team accountability to stick to agreements.
14. Energy and productivity are linked to good morale.
15. Collaboration relies on good team spirit. Team spirit relies on good morale.
16. Empowerment and individual potential must be nurtured.
17. Embrace diversity.
18. Draw on individual strengths. Allow team members to express themselves.
19. Constantly stretch beyond comfortable to true interdependent mastery.
20. Create, maintain, and evolve the prevailing climate to unlock full potential.

DASHBOARD
ACCELERATORS TO AUTOMATIC

This book effectively identifies, and then explains the critical elements of a winning mindset, a proven method, and an optimal mood, for sustained high performance. I have drawn on personal anecdotes as well as famous examples to reinforce where you or your team needs to focus if you are interested in accelerating from where you are now, to a situation where these elements are automatic.

The checklists below are summarised at the end of each section, but they are brought together here as a set of dials that really need to be on the same dashboard in order to achieve mastery, and to accelerate automatic achievement.

Mindset

1. Develop a growth mindset.
2. Practice servant leadership.
3. Find work that you enjoy.
4. Show up; anything worth doing is worth doing well.
5. Create a clear vision that you and your team believe in. Focus to manifest it.
6. Be yourself. Don't try to be someone else.
7. Earn respect by doing what you say you will. Serve the team.
8. Be an optimist.
9. Model consistently what you want to see in others.
10. Be honest about your shortcomings.
11. Consider the bigger picture. Serve the greater good.
12. Identify reference points for inspiration; personal and meaningful.
13. Be clear about your why; inspire others who believe what you believe.
14. Apply experiential learning.
15. Forgive others; it breaks down barriers.
16. Car dashboard fuel gauge: 10 per cent still in the tank at "empty".
17. Kennedy: Put a man on the moon.
18. Kipchoge and Bannister: Run through the perceived barrier.
19. Mandela: "It always seems impossible until it is done."
20. Lincoln: Never give up; success could be around the corner.

Method

1. Identify your accountability partners. Consider a coach.
2. Ensure excellent facilitation of team workshops.
3. Start as you mean to go on.
4. Do the right thing.
5. Do what you agree and commit to do.
6. World-class people maintain the highest standards no matter what.
7. Successful people stick to proven habits and routines.
8. Familiar routines promote focus and composure.
9. Chosen productive time needs to be the best time for you.
10. Learning is important for everyone at every level of the operation.
11. Create the correct surroundings and conditions for high performance.
12. Marginal gains and incremental change will lead to step change.
13. Take a disciplined approach to procedural adjustments.
14. Identify and capture inefficiencies and then work team solutions.
15. Invest in a visual platform to share knowledge.
16. Risks and lessons should be captured and worked to closure for the future.
17. Measure, illustrate, and display performance, even if the news is not positive.
18. Draw on team diversity, innovation, and creativity to continuously improve.
19. Recognise team members for a job well done.

20. Treat effective communication as the competitive advantage it is!

Mood

1. Drucker: "Culture eats strategy for breakfast!"
2. The most significant element is the sense of community.
3. Create the conditions for excellence. One team, one mission.
4. Build a sense of belonging.
5. Encourage collective contribution to vision and values.
6. Clear and visible charter of organisational purpose—your why.
7. Shared ownership of outcomes.
8. CrossFit: "Leave your ego at the door."
9. Be positive and avoid negative talk.
10. Listen to hear and understand.
11. Promote situational awareness from everyone.
12. Give everyone a voice.
13. Encourage team accountability to stick to agreements.
14. Energy and productivity are linked to good morale.
15. Collaboration relies on good team spirit. Team spirit relies on good morale.
16. Empowerment and individual potential must be nurtured.
17. Embrace diversity.
18. Draw on individual strengths. Allow team members to express themselves.
19. Constantly stretch beyond comfortable to true interdependent mastery.

20. Create, maintain, and evolve the prevailing climate to unlock full potential.

Model

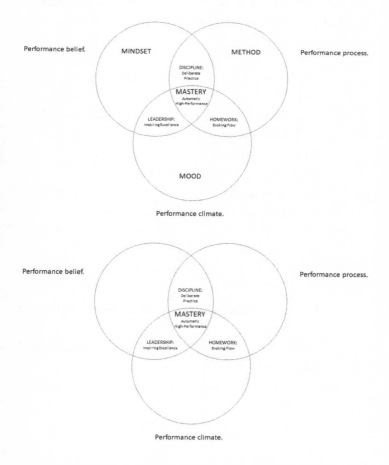

3M Model to Master Team and Individual Performance, by Tim Wigham, 2020.

Discipline—The Connection between Mindset and Method

Discipline means getting deliberate about turning a thought into an action. It therefore connects the mind with the activities necessary to unlock potential and to manifest a new reality.

1. Show up; anything worth doing is worth doing well.
2. Create a clear vision that you and your team believe in. Focus.
3. Be yourself. Don't try to be someone else.
4. Earn respect by doing what you say you will, when you say you will.
5. Do what you agree and commit to do.
6. World-class people maintain the highest standards no matter what.
7. Successful people stick to proven habits and routines.
8. Chosen productive time needs to be the best time for you.
9. Take a disciplined approach to procedural adjustments.
10. Identify and capture inefficiencies and then work on solutions.

Leadership—The Connection between Mindset and Mood

Self-leadership and team-leadership is fundamental in driving the right mindset, as well as in creating the conditions for excellence. Leadership therefore connects the mind with the necessary setting for optimal expression.

1. Practice servant leadership.
2. Identify reference points for inspiration; personal and meaningful.
3. Be clear about your why and inspire others who believe what you believe.
4. Forgive others; it breaks down barriers.
5. Kennedy: Put a man on the moon.
6. Mandela: "It always seems impossible until it is done."
7. Clear and visible charter of organisational purpose— your why.
8. Empowerment and individual potential must be nurtured.
9. Give everyone a voice.
10. Be honourable.

Teamwork or Homework—The Connection between Method and Mood

Teamwork or homework can be challenging, but when either achieves a state of flow, it is essentially unleashing the best of the team, or of your brain. Flow means to be in the zone or productively immersed in the task. Teamwork therefore appropriately connects the play with the playground and benefits most when both are optimal.

1. High-performing teams are safe teams.
2. Draw on team diversity, innovation, and creativity to continuously improve.
3. Effective communication is a competitive advantage in any team.
4. Drucker: "Culture eats strategy for breakfast!"
5. The most significant element is the sense of community.
6. Build a sense of belonging.
7. One team, one mission.
8. Collective contribution to vision and values.
9. Collaboration relies on good team spirit. Team spirit relies on good morale.
10. Embrace diversity.

Conclusion

I have had the privilege to support dozens of team campaigns. They have all had their adversity and achievement. They have all demonstrated significant improvement, and they have all taught me new lessons which have led me to write this guidebook about a simple model for creating the conditions to unlock excellence.

What has been reinforced for me time and time again is that successful campaigns require the right mindset, the right method, and the right mood.

Mindset is led by leadership! It involves openness to possibility, openness to objective assessment, openness to coaching, and a belief in better. It includes optimism and resilience in equal measure. Mindset is critical for initiative, which is then essential for acceleration to automatic.

Method is system discipline. It requires an uncompromising adherence to proven process even when it is the last thing anyone feels like doing. The process may not be perfect, but it certainly works. Method allows repeated practice to become automatic.

Mood describes the prevailing performance climate. It includes intangible but invaluable behaviours and deliverables which maintain the right atmosphere for team excellence. Mood is the magic which helps mindset and method to move mountains.

These three *M*s need to be tailored for each campaign. Subtle tweaks are needed because people are all different, and teams contain different people. However, accelerated improvement depends on the right mindset, requires a methodology which systemises and automates the improvement process, and thrives in a mood conducive to rapid transformation.

Mindset is a key part of the methodology, but it is also a prerequisite. Mood is also part of the method but warrants distinct explanation too. The three *M*s are effectively interwoven, and if interwoven effectively, they do reveal mastery.

Model: The best way to use the model for yourself or your team is to personalise it. Note what you have found to work best to lead the right mindset, drive the right method, and create the right mood. These elements then fuel accelerated performance and reveal mastery much sooner than might be the case if improvement is allowed to take its own slow time.

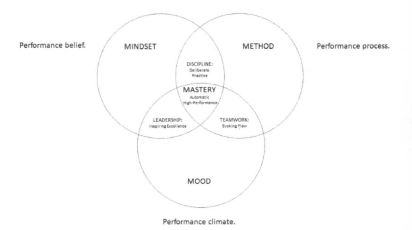

140

Accelerate your journey to mastery by noting your thoughts in the corresponding circles below. Visit www.inspired-books.com for a downloadable one-page PDF which includes all checklists and a large Venn diagram which can be used for a team, or individual brainstorm, to identify your specific triggers, behaviours, language, and aspirations, in each circle.

I recommend you complete a 3M model of your current realty, then a 3M model of your desired future state. After that, complete the accelerator between current reality and desired state to focus on exactly what you will do to master automatic excellence. This visual can then be tied into your goal-setting process for performance improvement. Remember to set SMART goals which are specific, measurable, attainable, relevant, and time-bound.

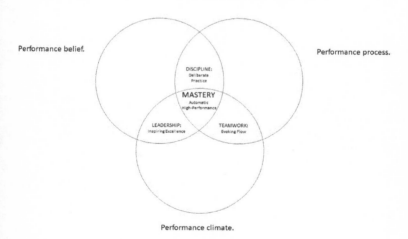

Performance belief.

Performance process.

DISCIPLINE:
Deliberate
Practice

MASTERY
Automatic
High-Performance

LEADERSHIP:
Inspiring Excellence

TEAMWORK:
Evoking Flow

Performance climate.

About the Author

Tim Wigham grew up in Southern Africa and has dual British and South African citizenship. He served in the British Commandos for eight years between 1992 and 2000 before completing his full-time MBA in Cape Town in 2001.

Tim specialised in the facilitation of SME executive leadership breakaways across a range of industries to build strong cohesion, clear strategy, mission, vision, and authentic company values.

In the sports industry, Tim worked on mental toughness with several of the Springbok rugby players who went on to be World Cup winners in 2007.

Tim is currently the head of performance improvement at Exceed in Aberdeen, Scotland. He has worked as a performance improvement expert in the energy sector since 2007.

Tim is based in the North East of Scotland; he is married and has three young children. His main interests include Christianity, family, fitness, reading, writing, and learning. He also enjoys blogging about inspiration.

About the Book

After reading scores of books on leadership, teamwork, discipline, and indeed performance, I now recognise various patterns and consistencies.

I spent three years capturing weekly insights, so my aim with this book was to place those insights into some sort of logical order based on my intuition, and based on the empirical data received from observations, analysis, clients and colleagues on team campaigns at the front line in various different settings.

I have always been interested in developing a user-friendly model which will help individuals and teams to accelerate their journey from average to automatic, and by automatic I mean an approach which is habitual and sustainable because it has accounted for the main aspects we can control for our own performance improvement. Furthermore, I wanted to distil from the data, several checklists which can help us all to understand what specifically aids the acceleration!

It is clear when you study or support champions or champion teams, that they dial in three critical success factors regarding what they can control. The first is the right mindset, the second is the right method or system, and the third is always a controlled preparation and learning climate (mood), with ideal conditions for optimal performance.

The global COVID-19 pandemic which is sweeping across our planet in 2020 may bring change, but a guaranteed constant will be what we can control in order to adapt to that change. This will most certainly include mastering the right mindset, the right method, and the right mood. Whether face-to-face, or virtually, we will also still need leadership, teamwork/homework, and discipline.

This book is an attempt to explore, integrate, and then connect mindset, method, and mood, so that we can master high performance for ourselves and our teams.

Bibliography

Bathla, S. *The Magic of Accelerated Learning: Discover Strategies for Effective Learning, Improved Memorisation, Sharpened Focus and Become an Expert in Any Skill You Want* (Create Space Independent Publishing, 2018).

Bergeron, B. *Chasing Excellence: A Story about Building the World's Fittest Athletes* (Lioncrest Publishing, 2017).

Brown, L., *The Best of Les Brown Audio Collection: Inspiration from the World's Leading Motivational Speaker* (Audible, 2016).

Chandler, S., and Litvin, R. *The Prosperous Coach: Increase Income and Impact for You and Your Clients* (Maurice Bassett, 2013).

Collins, J. *Good to Great: Why Some Companies Make the Leap, and Others Don't* (William Collins, 2001).

Covey, S. *The 7 Habits of Highly Effective People: Powerful Lessons in Personal Change* (Free Press, 1989).

Crabtree, S. Worldwide, 13% of Employees Are Engaged at Work: Low workplace engagement offers opportunities to improve business outcomes (2013)

De Sena, J. *The Spartan Way: Eat better. Train better. Think better. Be Better* (Barnes and Noble, 2018).

Duckworth, A. *Grit: The Power of Passion and Perseverance* (Scribner Book Company, 2016).

Gallwey, T. *The Inner Game of Work: Overcoming Mental Obstacles for Maximum Performance* (Texere Publishing, 2000).

Keane, B. *The Fitness Mindset: Eat for Energy, Train for Tension, Manage Your Mindset, Reap the Results* (Rethink Press Limited, 2018).

Larson, G. *The Far Side: 2nd First Look* (Andrews, McMeel and Parker, 1986).

Nicklas, C. *Create Your Story: Journal* (28 Quest, 2018).

Nelson Bolles, R. *What Colour Is Your Parachute: The Bestselling Job Hunting Book in the World* (Ten Speed Press, 1972).

Reed, R. *If I Could Tell You Just One Thing; Encounters with Remarkable People and Their Most Valuable Advice* (Chronicle Books, 2018).

Rothstein, L., and Budd, M. *You Are What You Say: The Proven Program That Uses the Power of Language to Combat Stress, Anger, and Depression* (Harmony, 2001).

Sinek, S. *Start with Why: How Great Leaders Inspire Everyone to Take Action* (Penguin books, 2009).

Stulberg, B., and Magness, S. *Peak Performance: Elevate Your Game, Avoid Burnout, and Thrive with the New Science of Success* (Rodale Books, 2017).

Syed, M. *Black Box Thinking* (John Murray, 2015).

Whitmore, J. *Coaching for Performance: The Principles and Practice of Coaching and Leadership* (Hodder and Stoughton, 2017).

Wigham, T. *!nspired: Performance Coaching Insights from the Front Line* (Author House, 2017).

---. *!nspired Too: More Performance Coaching Insights from the Front Line* (Author House, 2018).

---. *!nspired Again: More Performance Coaching Insights to Fuel your Fire* (Author House, 2019).

Willink, J., and Babin, L. *Extreme Ownership: How US Navy SEALS Lead and Win* (St Martin's Press, 2017).